FOCUS ON SUCCESS

Ausgabe Technik

The new edition

Workbook

CONTENTS

Free-time activities

1 FREE-TIME ACTIVITIES

›› SB page 6, exercise 1

Read the speech bubbles and name the speaker's free time activity.

1 *Well, it can be a bit boring but when you do catch something, wow!* ________

2 *I don't have a horse of my own. I have to borrow one.* ________

3 *Second-hand stuff is really cheap and we have a good free library in town, too.* ________

4 *I never bet money. No way. I play online for fun, but I play to win, of course.* ________

5 *Fridays and Saturdays I meet some mates and we dance the night away.* ________

6 *I don't just listen to music. I'm more creative. I generally write my own.* ________

2 PREPOSITIONS

›› SB page 7, text

Complete the text with words and phrases from the box. Use each word/phrase once only.

about | against | around | at | for | in | in front of | off | out | out of | round | with

Many people think that young people today only spend their free time sitting ________[1] the television. But do they really know what they are talking ________[2]? Chilling ________[3] and hanging ________[4] with friends are the favourite free-time activities, according to a new survey published today. Girls like looking ________[5] shops more than boys; they are more likely to be playing ________[6] other players online. Many young people do sport and play ________[7] teams; for them it is difficult to go clubbing ________[8] the weekend, otherwise they might find themselves ________[9] the team. Some young people also do something worthwhile, like working ________[10] a charity. Working ________[11] homeless people may not be everybody's idea of fun, but they obviously get a lot ________[12] it.

3 SUBJECT AND OBJECT PRONOUNS

›› SB page 8, exercise 5

Fill in the missing pronouns.

1 Sorry. Can ________[1] say that again? ________[2] didn't understand ________[3].

2 Do ________[1] know Tom Webb? ________[2] met ________[3] yesterday. ________[4]' s a champion dancer.

3 Don't give bread to the ducks. ________[1] says on that notice that ________[2]'s bad for ________[3].

4 Where are Janna and Josh? ________[1] told ________[2] not to be late because ________[3] must pick up our tickets by 8 o'clock or we lose ________[4].

5 Franzi's parents are too tolerant. ________[1]'s clear to ________[2] that ________[3] have a big problem with ________[4].

6 Sarah is worried about her son. ________[1] told ________[2] to work harder or ________[3] will have to take his exams again.

4 SIMPLE PRESENT

›› SB page 9, exercise 6

Use the elements to make complete sentences. Add any missing words.

1 Dana / do / voluntary work / three evenings / week

2 Ravi / be / football club / and / play / first team

3 Ravi and Jack / enjoy / clubbing but / not go / very often

4 how often / Lucy + go / work / each week / ?

5 Sal and Sam / not play / violent games /. They / prefer / test / their skill

6 you + have / a lot of free time / or / you + work / ?

5 PRESENT PROGRESSIVE

›› SB page 10, exercise 7

Use an expression from box A and a verb from box B to say what the people and animals are doing.

A ~~at the kiosk~~ | from a diving board | in blue boxer shorts | near some steps | on a bistro table | on a mobile phone | on a red blanket | a sunlounger (*Sonnenliege*) | out of the pool | under a tree

B ~~buy~~ | climb | dive | have (a picnic) | have (a shower) | jump | read | stand | sunbathe | talk

A man is buying an ice cream at the kiosk.

6 SIMPLE PRESENT OR PRESENT PROGRESSIVE?

›› SB pages 9–11

Cross out the incorrect form.

1 I am going / go to the fitness centre on Saturdays.
2 Alan is often reading / often reads two books a week.
3 Elle can't come to the phone now. She has / is having a shower.
4 We always do / are always doing[1] our homework as soon as we are getting / get[2] home.
5 Are you sometimes eating / Do you sometimes eat Indian food?
6 I am not liking / don't like our new neighbours much.
7 Do you plan / Are you planning a LAN party at the moment?
8 How much coffee are you drinking / do you drink a day?
9 Look! The sun comes / is coming out.
10 Sam prefers / is preferring games that test his skill.

7 SIMPLE PRESENT OR PRESENT PROGRESSIVE?

›› SB pages 9–11

Complete the sentences with the correct form of the verb in brackets.

1 Dana ____________[1] (spend) most of her free time working with the Red Cross. This week she ____________[2] (work) with homeless people. Her brother ____________[3] (not/think) she ____________[4] (enjoy) life.
2 Lucy ____________[1] (work) three evenings a week, but this evening she ____________[2] (do) her homework. She always ____________[3] (enjoy) going shopping with her friends.
3 Ravi usually ____________[1] (have) matches at the weekend. When he ____________[2] (not/play) football he ____________[3] (hang) around with his friends.

8 WORDFIELD: FREE-TIME ACTIVITIES

›› SB pages 6–7

Make a mindmap like the one below. Add as many different free-time activities as you can. Use your exercise book if necessary.

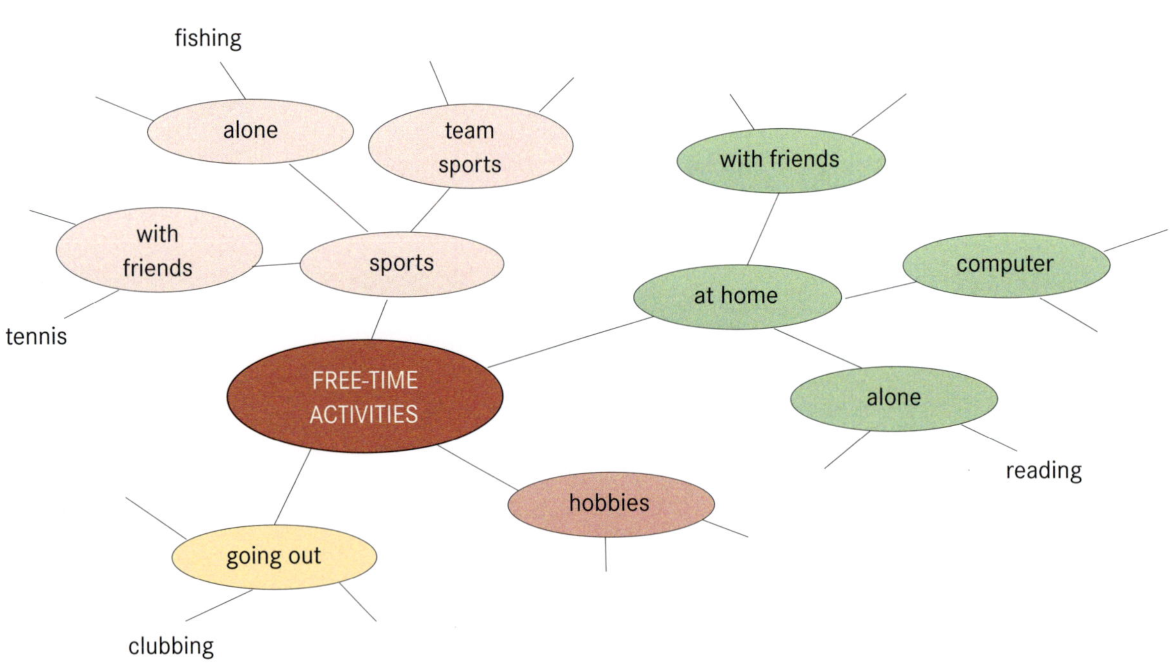

Girls fight for their rights

1 QUESTIONS AND ANSWERS

›› SB page 12, text

Match the questions 1–8 with the answers a–h.

1 How did Ashley's male teammates react at first? [f]
2 How do we know that Ashley's fans see her as a real fighter? [ ]
3 There are not enough girls to make up an all-girl team. What's the solution? [ ]
4 What do you understand by "Title IX"? [ ]
5 What does Ashley mean by "equal in every way"? [ ]
6 What is a girl's biggest problem about doing mixed sport? [ ]
7 What was Ashley Moore's "awesome challenge"? [ ]
8 Why did Ashley's opponent lose the match? [ ]

a Although the boy was big and strong, he was slow.
b She means that her male opponents should fight her exactly as they would fight a boy.
c In that case, girls have to join boys' teams.
d It's overcoming chauvinistic stereotyping.
e She had to wrestle a big boy from her school's most dangerous rival.
f Some just stared at her; others made nasty jokes.
g They compare her to Xena, a fictional warrior princess.
h Title IX is a federal law against sex discrimination in US public schools.

2 WORD SEARCH

›› SB page 12, text

Underline ten English words about sport that are used in the text. They are not necessarily in the same order.

3 THE SIMPLE PAST

›› SB page 14, exercise 3

Complete the sentences with the simple past form of the underlined verb. Be careful with irregular forms.

1 We normally train on Thursdays, but last week we ______________ on Wednesday.
2 Pete doesn't often win, but he ______________ his fight yesterday evening.
3 **A** Did you come to training by bike? **B** No, I ______________ by bus.
4 **A** Did you wear your new football boots for the match? **B** No, I ______________ my old ones.
5 **A** Did you buy that football shirt at Intersport? **B** No, I ______________ it online. It was cheaper.
6 **A** Did the trainer choose you for the first team? **B** Yes, but he ______________ me to play in goal.
7 **A** Did Ashley take part in the tournament last weekend? **B** Yes, she did. She ______________ part on both days.
8 **A** What time did you arrive here? **B** I ______________ at about two o'clock, I think.

4 NEGATIVES IN THE SIMPLE PAST

›› SB page 14, exercise 3

Look at the drawings and complete the sentence. Choose a verb from the box.

buy | go | have | meet | play | score | take | watch

1 

I *didn't watch TV* last night. I ______________.

2 

We ______________ clubbing on Saturday.
We ______________ to the movies.

3 

Jane ______________.
______________.

4 

They ______________.
______________.

5 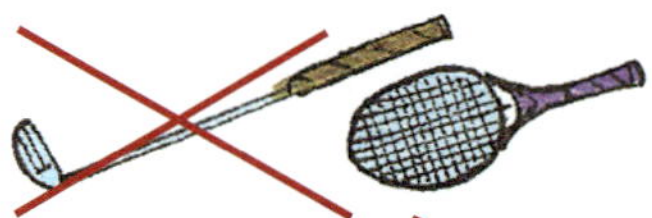

We ______________ yesterday.
______________.

6 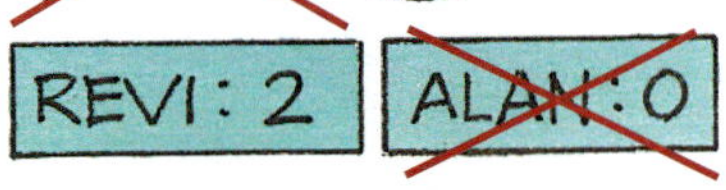

Alan ______________,
but Revi ______________.

7 Lucy  Sandra

Tom ______________ in town.
______________.

8 

I ______________ a laptop.
______________ a desktop computer.

5 ASKING QUESTIONS ABOUT THE PAST

›› SB page 14, exercise 3

Ask questions about the highlighted part of the sentences.

1 Josh and Janna went bowling last weekend.
When *did Josh and Janna go bowling* ?

2 Unfortunately, they missed their booking because of bad traffic delays.
Why ______________ ?

3 In the end, they waited for over two hours for a free lane (*Bahn*).
How long ______________ ?

4 They finally started their first game at 9 pm.
When ______________ their first game?

5 However, they became angry because their lane did not work properly.
Why ______________ ?

6 Josh complained to the manager about the faulty lane.
Who ______________ the faulty lane?

7 But the problem with this was that they had to wait a long time again.
What ______________ ?

8 Poor Josh and Janna finally arrived home at 2 o'clock in the morning.
When ______________ ?

C Refresher Course
You are what you eat

1 IN A RESTAURANT

›› SB page 16, text

Link the waiter's questions 1–8 to the diner's answers a–h.

1 How would you like your steak? [c]
2 May I show you our wine list? [ ]
3 What kind of water, please? [ ]
4 What would you like to drink? [ ]
5 Which kind of dressing would you like? [ ]
6 Would you like a dessert? [ ]
7 Would you like a starter? [ ]
8 Would you like to order now? [ ]

a I'll have a mineral water, please.
b Just oil and vinegar, please.
c Medium, please.
d No, thanks. We'll stay with non-alcoholic.
e No, thanks. We're all full to the top!
f Still, please.
g Yes, please. We're ready now.
h Yes, please. I'd like a small salad.

2 ODD WORD OUT

›› SB page 16, text

Which word does not fit? Use the words in the box to say why.

alcoholic drink | dessert | fish | fruit | meat | non-alcoholic/soft drink | nut | potato product | starter | vegetable

1 lamb cutlet | rump steak | scampi | schnitzel

The odd word out is ______________ because this is ______________ and not ______________ .

2 beer | orange juice | coke | mineral water

____

3 apples | kiwis | carrots | oranges

____

4 crisps | fries | peanuts | wedges

____

5 chocolate pudding | fruit salad | prawn cocktail | ice cream

____

3 POSSESSIVE ADJECTIVES

›› SB page 18, exercise 4

Complete the sentences.

__________[1] (My/I/Mine) brother lives in Los Angeles. __________[2] (He/His/He's) wife comes from Mexico. __________[3] (She/Her/She's) parents emigrated to the USA when she was small. They have __________[4] (they/there/their) own restaurant. __________[5] (It's/It/Its) name is "The Mexican TacAway". The meals are big and not expensive, so you really get a good deal for __________[6] (you/your/you're) money. When we go to visit them it's __________[7] (we/us/our) favourite place to eat!

4 COUNTABLE AND UNCOUNTABLE NOUNS

›› SB page 19, exercise 5

Complete the sentences with *a/an* or *the*, only if necessary. If you don't need an article, write _x_ .

1 Do you want ________ ketchup on your chips?

2 Are you going to have ________[1] starter? – No, thanks. I think I'll just have ________[2] main course and then ________[3] dessert.

3 I love ________[1] ham and ________[2] eggs for ________[3] breakfast.

4 I hate ________[1] honey. I much prefer ________[2] bread and ________[3] butter with ________[4] jam.

5 I'm really full. I've just had ________[1] donut and ________[2] cappucino.

6 I'm going to buy ______ hamburger. I'm starving!

5 UNCOUNTABLE NOUNS

›› SB page 19, exercise 5

Complete the shopping list.

a _bit/piece_ of cheese	a ____________ of butter
two ____________ of chocolate	six ____________ of toilet paper
a ____________ of ketchup	two ____________ of peas
three ____________ of jam	a large ____________ of ice-cream
two ____________ of bread	a ____________ of toothpaste

6 UNCOUNTABLE NOUNS AND SINGULAR VERBS

›› SB page 19, exercise 5

Complete the sentences. Use the English translation of one of the words in box A and the correct form of one of the verbs in box B.

A Beweise | Informationen | Forschung | Möbel(stücke) | Rat(schläge) | Software

B be | come | cost | look | prove | show

1 The ______________________________ that the thief was a woman.

2 Her ______________________________ direct from the president herself.

3 Her ______________________________ based on her own experience.

4 The latest ______________________________ that the weather is getting warmer.

5 The new ______________________________ twice as much as the old software.

6 Her ____________________ really ____________ out of date.

7 SOME, ANY

›› SB page 20, exercise 6A

Fill in *some* or *any*.

1 **A** Would you like ___________[1] chips, Tom? **B** No, thanks. I never eat ___________[2] fried food.

2 **A** Jasmin, could you give me ___________[1] help in the kitchen, please? **B** Just a minute. I'm just getting ___________[2] carrots from the garden.

3 **A** Have you got ___________[1] mustard? **B** Well, we did have ___________[2] somewhere, but I can't find it now. I can borrow ___________[3] from our neighbour, if you want.

4 **A** I haven't got ___________[1] milk left. **B** OK, I'll go to shop and get ___________[2] .

8 SOMETHING/ANYTHING, SOMEBODY/ANYBODY, SOMEWHERE/ANYWHERE

›› SB page 20, exercise 6B

Cross out the incorrect form.

1 Is Cathy ill? She hasn't eaten anything / ~~something~~ all day.

2 It's awful. I must have left my coat anywhere / somewhere [1] in town. I can't find it anywhere / somewhere [2].

3 **A** Something / Anything [1] must have happened to John. He never comes home late without phoning me.
B I don't think something / anything [2] has happened to him. I think he's forgotten his mobile. I saw it somewhere / anywhere [3] a minute ago.

4 I've never heard anything / something so silly in my whole life!

5 I'm sorry. Ask anybody / somebody [1] else. I don't know anything / something [2] about computers.

6 **A** I read anywhere / somewhere [1] that sugar makes you stupid. **B** Yes, anybody / somebody [2] told me that, too. I hope he wasn't trying to tell me anything / something [3] because I was eating an ice-cream at the time!

9 MUCH, MANY, A LOT OF / PLENTY OF

›› SB page 21, exercise 6C

Cross out the incorrect form.

1 Hurry up, Lisa. We don't have ~~many~~ / much time.

2 How many / much TV does Harry watch a day?

3 Tom's new bike cost a lot of / much money.

4 Why did you buy so many / much [1] rolls? We have many / plenty of [2] bread already.

5 Did you see many / much people you know at the concert?

6 You needn't fill up the car. There's much / plenty of [1] petrol in the tank and we don't need many / much [2] litres to go to Leeds and back.

10 (A) LITTLE, (A) FEW

›› SB page 21, exercise 6D

Fill in *(a) few* or *(a) little*.

1 Can you give me _a little_ help with this, please?

2 A lot of young people have ___________ interest in good food.

3 **A** Nowadays, ___________[1] people can afford to eat out.
B I know. We have only sold ___________[2] meals so far today.

4 **A** Don't buy too much fish. Very ___________[1] people eat it. **B** OK, I'll just buy ___________[2] tuna.

5 I only have ___________ money with me. I'll pay with my card.

6 **A** A lot of fathers have ___________[1] time for their children, I'm afraid.
B And what about working mothers? People should think about them ___________[2] , too.

D Time out

1 WORKING WITH WORDS

›› SB page 22, text

Replace the words in brackets with a synonym from the box.

agrees with her parents | are against | attitude to | chance | details | exciting place | go to | planning to get a job | points out | sad | sensible | thinks

Holly's email gives us ______[1] (information) about her future plans. She wants to go to an ______[2] (exotic destination) like Brazil or India, but her parents ______[3] (won't agree to) this idea. Holly is ______[4] (unhappy) about her parents' ______[5] (opinion of) her plans. She ______[6] (feels) that she'll never have another ______[7] (opportunity) to ______[8] (visit) such places again. But Jala ______[9] (thinks that her parents are right). She ______[10] (says) that as Holly is ______[11] (going to work) for some of the time, it would be more ______[12] (reasonable) to go to an English-speaking country.

2 THE *WILL* FUTURE

›› SB page 24, exercise 4

Fill in the correct form of the *will* future.

1 **A** I hope it ______[1] (not rain) tomorrow. **B** Well, the forecast said it ______[2] (be) cloudy but dry.

2 ______ (you + help) me with my luggage, Tom? It's heavy.

3 I must go now or I ______ (miss)[1] my plane and then I ______[2] (be) in real trouble.

4 Don't worry, Mum. I ______[1] (not forget) to phone you as soon as I land in New York. I ______[2] (call) you on your mobile so you ______[3] (not need) to wait at home.

5 How long ______ (your flight + take), Holly?

6 Drive carefully or I ______ (never lend) you my car again, OK?

3 THE *GOING TO* FUTURE

›› SB page 24, exercise 4

Fill in the correct form of the *going to* future.

1 Holly's parents ______ (visit) her in the USA soon.

2 I ______ (arrange) my time out in the USA through Work America.

3 ______ (you + work) in the USA, Holly?

4 Most of my friends ______ (not take)[1] time out. They ______ (start)[2] work immediately.

5 ______ (Holly + have) time to see the sights?

6 Hurry up! Your plane ______ (take off) in a minute.

4 WHICH FUTURE FORM?

›› SB page 24, exercise 4

Cross out the incorrect form.

1 Are you going to go / Do you go to Holly's farewell party?

2 Is Holly really going to take / Does Holly really take time out?

3 I expect I 'm / 'll be [1] a bit late, I'm afraid. You 're having to start / 'll have to start [2] without me.

4 I hope we 're seeing / 'll see Josh and Janna at Holly's party

5 The mechanic told me that he 's finishing / 'll finish fixing the car by 5 o'clock.

6 Slow down! Can't you see that the cars in front are going to stop / will stop?

5 PRESENT PROGRESSIVE WITH FUTURE MEANING

›› SB page 24, exercise 4

Josh and Janna are talking about their plans for next weekend. Fill in the gaps in their conversation.

Janna: What ______________________ [1] (you + do) at the weekend, Josh?

Josh: I ______________________ [2] (you + go) to see my sister in Brighton.

Janna: Oh, yes. ______________________ [3] (go) alone?

Josh: No, my parents ______________________ [4] (come) with me and my brother ______________________ [5] (meet) us there, too. And what about you, Janna. ______________________ [6] (do) anything?

Janna: Well, I ______________________ [7] (not do) anything special. I ______________________ [8] (stay) at home because my mum and dad ______________________ [9] (visit) some friends in Oxford at the weekend.

Josh: Hey, that sounds good! I've just changed my mind. I ______________________ [10] (not go) to Brighton after all. I ______________________ [11] (spend) the weekend here with you.

6 TRAIN TIMES

›› SB page 24, exercise 4

Look at the timetable and complete the questions and answers.

	Abfahrt		Ankunft
Frankfurt (M)	6:00	Paris	9:50
Frankfurt (M)	9:01	Paris	12:49
Frankfurt (M)	13:01	Paris	16:50
Frankfurt (M)	19:01	Paris	22:53
Paris	6:58	Frankfurt (M)	10:58
Paris	9:09	Frankfurt (M)	12:58
Paris	13:09	Frankfurt (M)	16:58
Paris	19:05	Frankfurt (M)	22:58

TGV – train à grande vitesse
Paris-Est – Saarbrücken – Kaiserslautern – Mannheim – Frankfurt a. M.

1 What time does the first train to Paris ______________________ (leave) Frankfurt?
The first train to Paris ______________________ Frankfurt at ______________________ .

2 What time ______________________ (last train / Paris / arrive) in Frankfurt?
The ______________________ in Frankfurt at 22:58.

3 Where ______________________ (train / stop) inside Germany?
The train stops at ______________________ .

4 How long ______________________ (journey / take)?
The journey ______________________ .

Shopping

1 PUZZLE

›› SB page 26, text

Do the puzzle to find the key word.

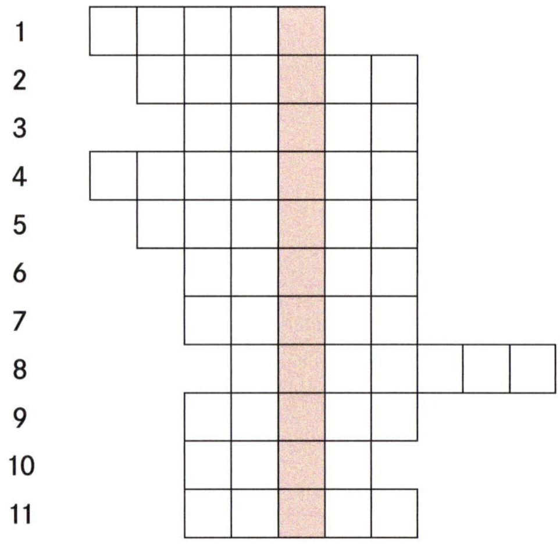

1 The people who serve you in a shop are the sales ... .
2 An Italian fashion designer whose name begins with A is ... .
3 Can't you take "No" for an answer? Don't be so ... .
4 Sharon's love of fashion and ... got her into debt.
5 Sharon did most of her shopping at eBay and at ... shops.
6 Another word for "shop" is "...".
7 Unfortunately, Sharon spent much more ... than she had.
8 I bought this shirt at half price. It was a real ... .
9 With designer clothes, the ... is often on the outside.
10 Sharon bought a ... cocktail dress on eBay.
11 A line of people waiting to be served is called a ... .

The key word is ______________________ .

2 ADJECTIVES

›› SB page 28, exercise 3

Find adjectives in the headlines below that match these German words.

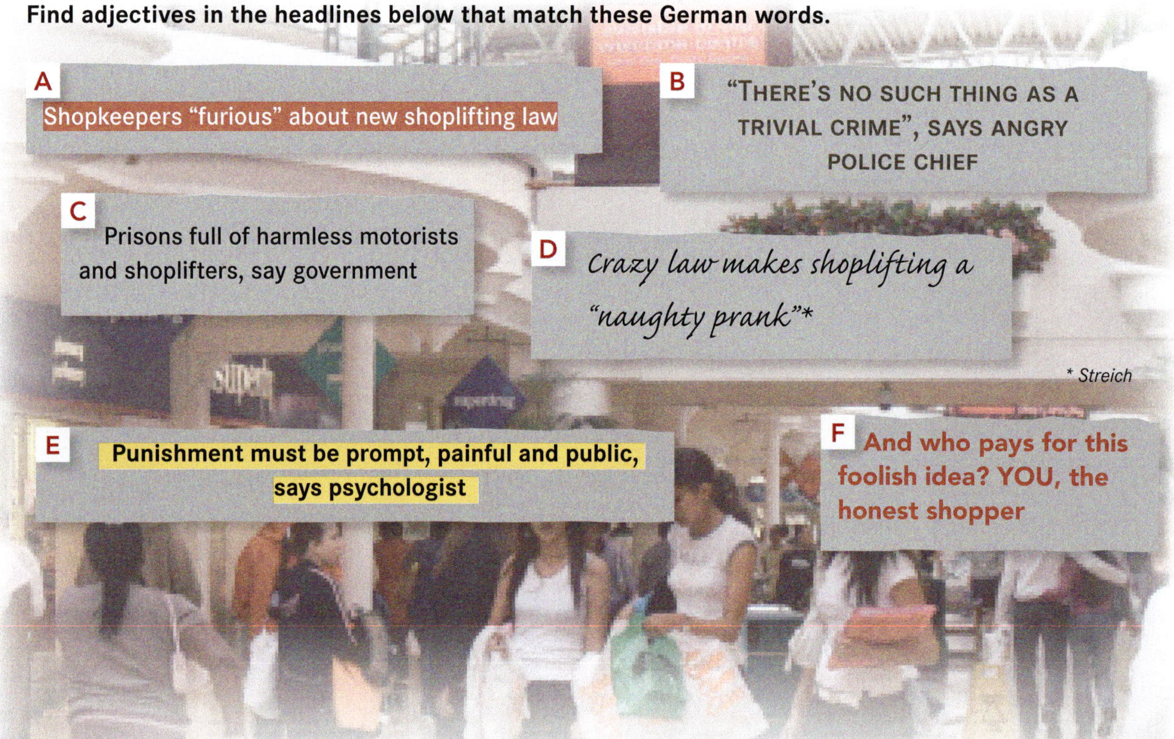

A Shopkeepers "furious" about new shoplifting law

B "THERE'S NO SUCH THING AS A TRIVIAL CRIME", SAYS ANGRY POLICE CHIEF

C Prisons full of harmless motorists and shoplifters, say government

D *Crazy law makes shoplifting a "naughty prank"**

* *Streich*

E Punishment must be prompt, painful and public, says psychologist

F And who pays for this foolish idea? YOU, the honest shopper

1 albern ______________
2 ehrlich ______________
3 erbost ______________
4 geringfügig ______________
5 harmlos ______________
6 neu ______________
7 öffentlich ______________
8 schmerzhaft ______________
9 ungezogen ______________
10 verrückt ______________
11 voll ______________
12 wütend ______________

3 ADVERBS

›› SB page 28, exercise 3

Rewrite the sentences. Use an adverb instead of an adjective.

1	Ali's English is very good.	Ali speaks English very ______.
2	Madison is a wonderful dancer.	Madison ______.
3	Simon is a fast runner.	Simon ______.
4	Helen is a careful driver.	Helen ______.
5	Accidents are always unexpected.	Accidents always happen ______.
6	Most people are hard workers.	Most ______.
7	Susan is a skillful painter.	Susan ______.
8	Jim is very bad at dancing.	Jim ______.

4 WHEN TO USE ADJECTIVES AND ADVERBS

›› SB page 28, exercise 3

Read the example sentences 1–6, then link them to the explanations a–f.

Example sentences		Explanations
1 Emma bought an exclusive dress on eBay.	c	a adjective qualifies *be/become/seem*
2 A lot of people are worried about money.		b adjective qualifies *feel/look* (= aussehen)/ *smell/taste*
3 The assistant smiled very pleasantly.		c adjective qualifies noun
4 The man looked closely at the phone.		d adverb qualifies adjective
5 This jacket is unusually good value for money.		e adverb qualifies adverb
6 Your perfume smells fabulous.		f adverb qualifies verb

5 TRANSLATION

›› SB page 29, exercise 4

Finish translating the sentences into English. Be careful about adverb order, too.

1 *Ich fühlte mich fürchterlich. Ich war fürchterlich müde.*

I felt ______. I was ______.

2 *Gewöhnlich hat sie ein ruhiges Leben. Gestern aber hatte sie ein ungewöhnliches Erlebnis.*

She ______.

But yesterday ______.

3 *Plötzlich hörte der Hund etwas. Das plötzliche Geräusch weckte ihn auf und er bellte los.*

The dog ______ something. The ______

______ and he began to bark.

4 *Die Musik war so laut, dass die Gäste sehr laut miteinander reden mussten.*

______ that the guests ______

______.

F Refresher Course
Ready for a job?

1 PHOTOS

›› SB page 30, questionnaire

Which questions in the questionnaire do the photos illustrate? Be careful: one photo doesn't fit at all.

1 ______

2 ______

3 ______

4 ______

5 ______

6 ______

7 ______

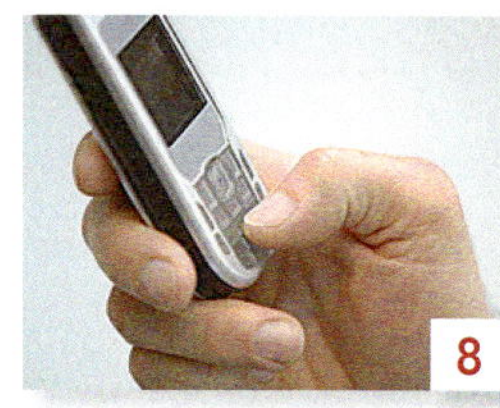
8 ______

2 JOBS

›› SB pages 30–32

Sort the jobs (box A) and the usual places of work (box B) into the correct column.

A baby-sitter | building worker | waiter | car-washer | cashier | courier rider | shop assistant | delivery boy/girl | dog-exerciser | gardener | kitchen help | shelf-filler

B building site | garage | garden | local park | private home | restaurant | self-service store | shop | street

indoor job	usual place of work	outdoor job	usual place of work
baby-sitter	*private home*		

3 PRESENT PERFECT

›› SB page 33, exercise 6

Use *has/have*, the correct form of the full verb or both.

1 Have you ______[1] (hear)? The Greens have just ______[2] (buy) a luxury caravan.

2 Have you ______ (switch) off the lights?

3 How long ______ Ben ______ (know) his girlfriend?

4 ______ the dog ______ (have) his walk yet?

5 Jack ______[1] (leave) school and ______[2] (get) a job.

6 We ______ just ______ (start) a new English book.

4 FOR, SINCE

›› SB page 34, exercise 6B

Put in *for* or *since*.

1 ______ two years
2 ______ she had a baby
3 ______ 2007
4 ______ a long time
5 ______ ages
6 ______ we moved to London
7 ______ several hours
8 ______ ever

5 THERE'S STILL WORK TO DO

›› SB page 33, exercise 6

Look at the drawings and say what the people still haven't done or haven't done yet. Be careful about word order.

1 I ______ the washing-up ______.
2 We ______ the car.
3 They ______ the cat ______.
4 Susan ______ the grass.
5 Kevin ______ face ______.
6 Tom ______ his homework.

6 SPOT THE MISTAKE

›› SB page 33, exercise 6

Cross out the incorrect form.

1 I 've lived / live here all my life.
2 We 've gone / went to the movies last night.
3 I'll help you when I finished / 've finished these emails.
4 Josh has cut / cut the grass yesterday.
5 Did you see / Have you seen Josh anywhere?
6 Susan still didn't phone / hasn't phoned.
7 I don't speak / haven't spoken to Holly for a long time.
8 Mum has told / tells you not to do that dozens of times.

7 TRANSLATION

›› SB page 33, exercise 6

Translate the sentences into English.

1 *Mein Kumpel hat eine neue Gitarre gekauft.*
My mate ______.
2 *Wir wohnen seit fünf Jahren in Deutschland.*
We ______.
3 *Hast du den neuesten Tom Hanks-Film gesehen?*
______ latest Tom Hanks ______?
4 *Ich habe meine Großeltern seit Weihnachten nicht mehr besucht.*
I ______.

City lights

1 PREPOSITIONS

›› SB page 37, text

Stefan has arrived in New York and is emailing an American friend. Cross out the incorrect prepositions.

Hi Paul

Well, here I am on / at / in [1] New York, and very soon I'll be seeing you in / on / at [2] Chicago. I'm looking forward at / to / into [3] that a lot!

I'm staying by / with / at [4] my cousin Krystal to / at / on [5] her little place on / up / at [6] the 11th floor in / at / of [7] an old apartment building near / under / over [8] Brooklyn Bridge.

Take a look at / into / by [9] the photo attachment. That's Krystal in / at / on [10] the right. I took the photo yesterday when we went on / by / up [11] the Empire State Building. The view through / down / over [12] Manhattan from / across / in [13] the top was fantastic! Thinking about / on / into [14] my trip to see you, I've been checking times and prices by / on / in [15] the internet, and I've decided to travel through / by / on [16] train, and I want to take the 06.45 at / in / on [17] Saturday. It'll get there at / in / on [18] 15.55. Will you be able to meet me on / through / at [19] the station?

Anyway, I must run now. Krystal and I are going to a party this evening, and she's going to introduce me with / to / around [20] all her friends.

See you soon. Stefan

2 BUILDING SKILLS: USING YOUR OWN WORDS

›› SB page 40, text

A Complete the tables with words from the Section B text.

Verb	Noun
breathe	______
______	exploration
construct	______
fail	______
recover	______

Noun	Adjective
distance	______
______	traditional
______	energetic
______	technological
______	free

B Use related words from A to rewrite the sentences, replacing the highlighted words.

1 In many New York neighbourhoods, street festivals are traditional.

In many neighbourhoods, there's a ____________________ of street festivals.

2 New York began constructing skyscrapers in the 1880s.

The ____________________ in New York began in the 1880s.

3 In the 1970s, New York failed to control drugs and crime.

In the 1970s, there was ____________________ .

4 The city took quite a long time to recover after that period.

After that period, the city's ____________________ .

5 Many immigrants to New York feel they are free to start life again.

Many immigrants to New York feel they have ____________________ .

3 COMPARISON OF ADJECTIVES

›› SB page 44, Grammar checkpoint

Ricky wants to buy a car, but he can only buy a cheap one. Study the table and complete his thoughts.

	Chico (1.2 petrol)	Star (1.5 petrol)	Delta (1.4 diesel)
fast	*	**	***
light	***	*	**
safe	*	**	***
expensive	*	**	***
economical	**	*	***
comfortable	*	**	***
powerful	*	***	**

(*** = most; * = least)

A Complete Ricky's thoughts about the Delta.

If I have to choose one of these cars, I'd better pick the 1.4-litre Delta. It's *the most expensive*[1] (expensive) option, but with its diesel engine it's ____________________[2] (economical) to run. It isn't *as powerful as*[3] (powerful) the Star. On the other hand, it's ____________________[4] (fast) than the Star because it's ____________________[5] (light). It's also ____________________[6] (safe) of all three cars, and it's ____________________[7] (comfortable), too.

B Complete Ricky's thoughts about the Chico.
(Note that some of the adjectives are the opposites of ones in the table.)

The car that I certainly wouldn't choose is the 1.2-litre Chico. Although it's ____________________[1] (cheap) of the three, it isn't ____________________[2] (economical) the Delta. What's more, think about all the bad points. Because it's ____________________[3] (light) of the three, it's also ____________________[4] (dangerous) of them all. In an accident, it would just fall to pieces! And its small 1.2 engine makes it ____________________[5] (slow) and ____________________[6] (powerful) of all three cars. It's also ____________________[7] (comfortable) of them all.

4 TOO ... AND (NOT) ... ENOUGH

›› SB page 44, Grammar checkpoint

It is summer, and Ricky wants to drive his 'new' car to Oregon and see Sue. (They are still good friends!) But his parents are not happy.

Mother: listen, that car (be) / old to drive across America

Listen, that car is too ______________________

____

______________________.

Father: yes, the car (not be) tough / to go all that way

Yes, the car isn't ______________________.

Mother: I agree: it (not be) reliable / for such a big trip

____

____

Father: I really think Oregon (be) / far for this old vehicle - and for you

____

____

Mother: yes, you (be) / young for something like this

____

____

Father: yes, you (not be) experienced / a journey across the USA

____

____

Mother: and think about the cost of fuel: it (be) / expensive now

____

____

Father: yes, ancient cars like this one (not be) economical /

____

____

5 PROBLEMS WITH COMPARISONS

›› SB page 44, Grammar checkpoint

Cross out the mistake in each sentence and write the correct word(s).

1 Is NY bigger ~~as~~ Berlin? *than*
2 New York is the most amazing city of the world. ______________
3 Manhattan is the famousest island in the world. ______________
4 San Francisco isn't as big like New York. ______________
5 Is San Francisco's Golden Gate Park so large as Central Park? ______________
6 Fifth Avenue isn't the same like the other streets of Manhattan: it is very special! ______________
7 The Brooklyn Bridge is more old than the Golden Gate Bridge. ______________

6 WORDFIELD: CITY LIFE

A Find 18 words in the word square.

S	A	P	A	R	T	M	E	N	T	W	S	K	Y	L	I	N	E	I	K	L	M	P	O	S
C	W	K	K	L	E	Z	T	R	A	S	S	B	G	M	J	S	H	O	P	P	I	N	G	K
O	X	N	N	E	I	G	H	B	O	U	R	H	O	O	D	S	T	B	K	E	P	T	H	Y
M	S	C	W	O	I	G	P	R	E	N	Y	U	L	Q	D	C	H	U	Y	T	Z	F	B	S
M	W	A	D	H	A	T	T	R	A	C	T	I	O	N	K	R	M	I	O	R	I	E	L	C
U	C	P	N	B	M	T	W	V	X	K	V	C	B	R	U	O	L	L	N	A	B	S	T	R
N	E	I	Z	O	B	E	D	O	W	N	T	O	W	N	I	W	O	D	M	F	P	T	K	A
I	M	T	I	R	I	N	R	G	H	T	J	K	Y	E	U	D	E	I	G	F	J	I	R	P
T	K	A	L	O	R	E	M	B	U	S	I	N	E	S	S	E	Z	N	O	I	U	V	N	E
Y	P	L	W	U	E	R	V	I	O	M	Z	R	K	T	N	D	R	G	M	C	E	A	W	R
J	T	E	I	G	F	G	H	C	U	L	T	U	R	A	L	A	W	A	E	H	D	L	I	N
M	A	S	G	H	E	Y	T	P	F	I	O	N	T	W	G	T	R	A	D	I	T	I	O	N

B Now complete the following sentences with words from the word square.

1 New York is not the ______________________ of New York State; that is Albany.

2 New York has five ______________________: Manhattan, the Bronx, Queens, Brooklyn and Staten Island.

3 The Empire State ______________________[1] is one of the most famous ______________________[2] in New York.

4 The Statue of Liberty is a popular tourist ______________________ .

5 The streets in Manhattan are ______________________[1] day and night with ______________________[2]. It takes hours to drive anywhere.

6 There is a very large Chinese ______________________ in Chinatown.

7 TECHNICAL OPTIONS

›› SB page 43

Mediation: Sie möchten jemandem auf Englisch sagen, dass ...

1 ... Unfälle und schlechtes Wetter häufige Ursachen für lange Staus auf den Autobahnen sind.

____

____

2 ... ein Verkehrsleitsystem nur funktionieren kann, wenn alle Fahrer die empfohlene Geschwindigkeit einhalten.

____

____

3 ... bei diesem System, die Verkehrsdichte durch Loop-Detektoren unter (*beneath*) der Straßenoberfläche gemessen wird.

____

____

4 ... wenn der Stau sich auflöst, das Leitsystem sich automatisch abschaltet.

____

____

2 Advertising

1 OPPOSITES

›› SB page 46, text

A Find opposites of the following in the text.

1 past ______
2 offline ______
3 complicated ______
4 no-one ______
5 shrinking ______
6 end ______
7 excluding ______
8 separately ______

B Use pairs of opposites from A to complete the following.

1 After you've found the material you need on the internet, you don't need to stay ______[1] . You can download it and work on it ______[2].

2 People are reading newspapers less these days, so sales are ______[1] . However, use of newspaper websites is ______[2] .

3 "______[1] will be at the office at 6.30 a.m.," I thought. But I was wrong. When I arrived, ______[2] was already there!

4 The bill for the campaign came to £2.3m, ______[1] media costs, but ______[2] tax. That was an extra £400,000!

2 PAST PROGRESSIVE AND SIMPLE PAST

›› SB page 54, Grammar checkpoint

Make sentences with the correct form of the verbs.
Use *when* with 'short' actions.
Use *while* with 'long' actions.

The journey to Ibiza

1 / sun (rise) / Mandy (get) taxi / airport – *when*

The sun was rising when Mandy got a taxi to the airport.

2 everything / (go) well / suddenly (have) a puncture (*= Reifenpanne*) – *when*

______

3 / (look) at her watch / taxi driver (change) the wheel – *while*
She was going to be late!

______

4 / (start) again / roads (get) very busy with the morning rush hour – *when*

______

______

5 they (call) / flight for / last time / she finally (check in) – *when*

______

6 / (run) to / gate / (see) her friend Alice by / gate and (wave) – *while*

____

7 / (still explain) her terrible journey / they (get) on the plane – *when*

____

8 And that was not the end of it! / (fly) into a terrible storm / they (come down) to land in Ibiza – *while*

____

9 / (wait) for a bus / their hotel / (get) wet and cold in / rain – *while*

____

10 But thank goodness! / sun (come out) / they (drive) / the hotel – *while*

____

And it stayed warm for the whole of their holiday.

3 RELATIVE CLAUSES AND CONTACT CLAUSES

›› SB page 54, Grammar checkpoint

Complete these parts of classified ads in a local newspaper. Add *who*, *which* or *that* only where necessary. If unnecessary, write X.

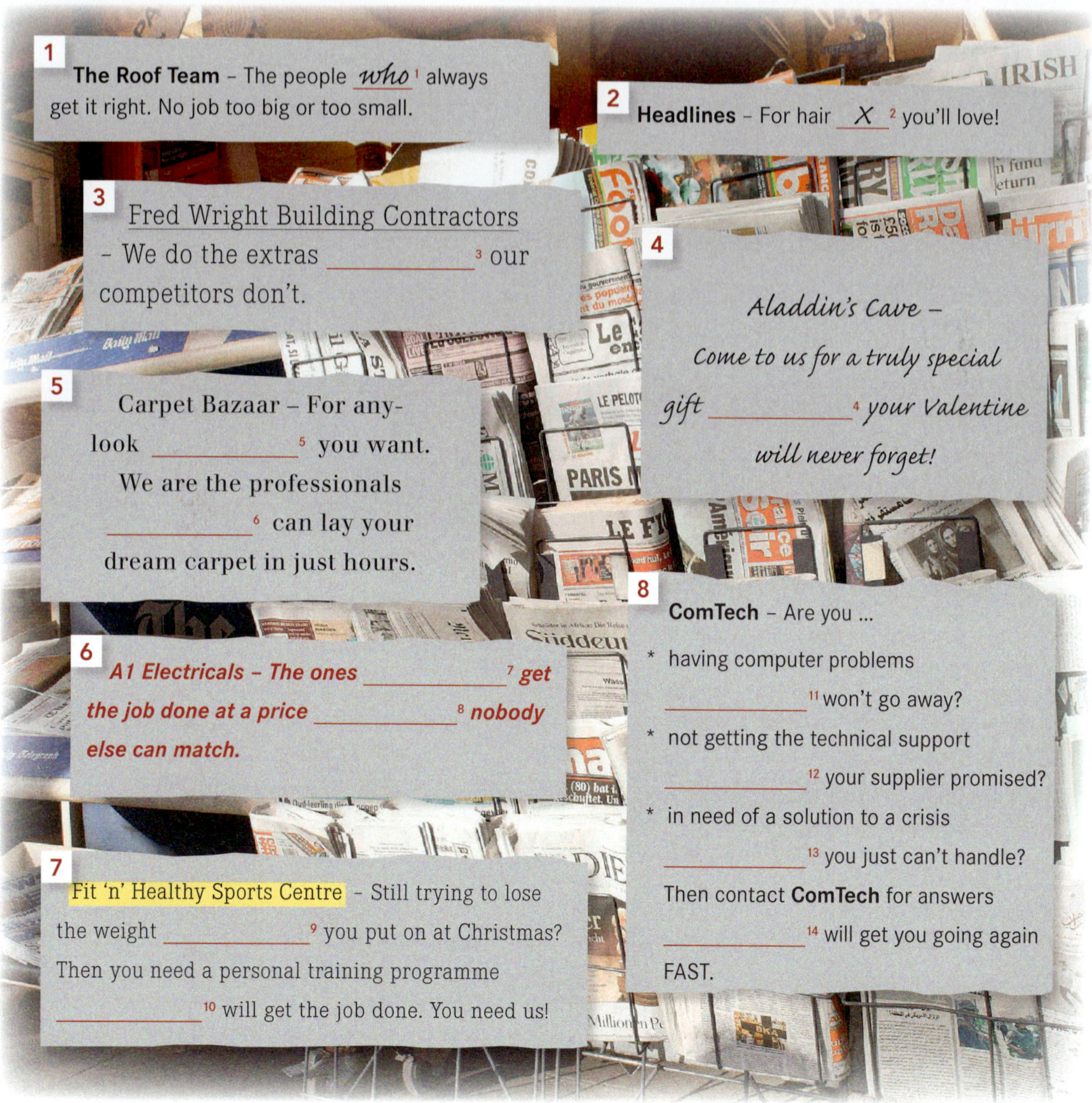

1 **The Roof Team** – The people *who*[1] always get it right. No job too big or too small.

2 **Headlines** – For hair *X*[2] you'll love!

3 Fred Wright Building Contractors – We do the extras __________[3] our competitors don't.

4 *Aladdin's Cave – Come to us for a truly special gift __________[4] your Valentine will never forget!*

5 Carpet Bazaar – For any-look __________[5] you want. We are the professionals __________[6] can lay your dream carpet in just hours.

6 ***A1 Electricals – The ones __________[7] get the job done at a price __________[8] nobody else can match.***

7 Fit 'n' Healthy Sports Centre – Still trying to lose the weight __________[9] you put on at Christmas? Then you need a personal training programme __________[10] will get the job done. You need us!

8 **ComTech** – Are you …

* having computer problems __________[11] won't go away?
* not getting the technical support __________[12] your supplier promised?
* in need of a solution to a crisis __________[13] you just can't handle?

Then contact **ComTech** for answers __________[14] will get you going again FAST.

4 BUILDING SKILLS: ANALYZING CHARTS

A Look at the chart, read the analysis and name the country:

____

GDP rose steadily between 2002 and 2004. Then there was a slight decline from 2004-2006. Following that, it remained flat in 2006-7 before a sharp rise during 2008.

B Rewrite the analysis in A. Use alternative forms as much as you can.

There was a steady rise in GDP from 2002–2004.

After that, it declined

____

C Now write about Germany between 1996 and 2002.

____

____

____

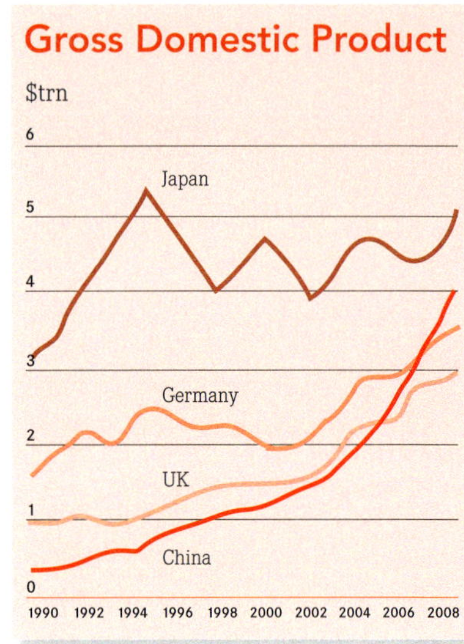

Source: *The Economist*

5 WORDFIELD: ADVERTISING

Do the crossword puzzle.

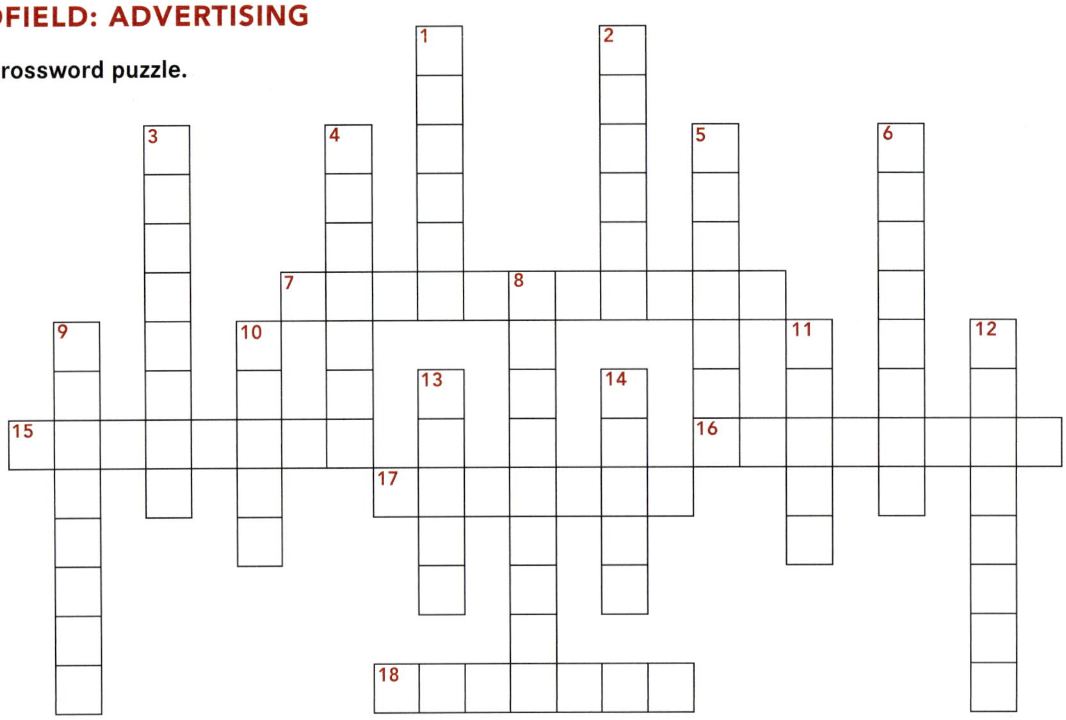

Across

7 This is the subject of Unit 2.
15 a business agreement
16 a person who makes products look their best
17 A media ... decides where and when to advertise.
18 the companies that an advertising agency works for

Down

1 You can have apple or pineapple juice. It's your ...
2 pictures
3 ... are often just made from A4 paper folded once.
4 the thing that an advertiser advertises
5 ... goods sell well because people trust the name.
6 a programme of advertising to introduce something new
8 Product placement is a clever advertising ...
9 You'll find your perfect holiday in our beautiful, new ... !
10 Look at the ... and you'll see that the company has grown fast.
11 The high ... of TV advertising make it very expensive.
12 Somebody who thinks of words or images to sell a product
13 the results of selling
14 How much money did the company ... on advertising last year?

6 TECHNICAL OPTIONS

›› SB page 53

A Read the text and put the correct captions beneath the photos.

1 

2 

3 

4 

______ ______ ______ ______

There are four main types of light source, two incandescent and two fluorescent. The most common incandescent bulbs are the ordinary Edison bulb and the halogen bulb, which is an improvement on Edison's invention. However, both these bulbs are very inefficient. Most of the electricity they consume is not converted into light at all, but into excess heat – in the case of Edison's bulb, almost 90%, in fact.

Tubular fluorescent bulbs are designed to solve the problem of wasting electricity in the form of excess heat. The most common light sources that use this technology are strip lighting and CFLs.

B Read the description of the structure of an Edison bulb and label the drawing.

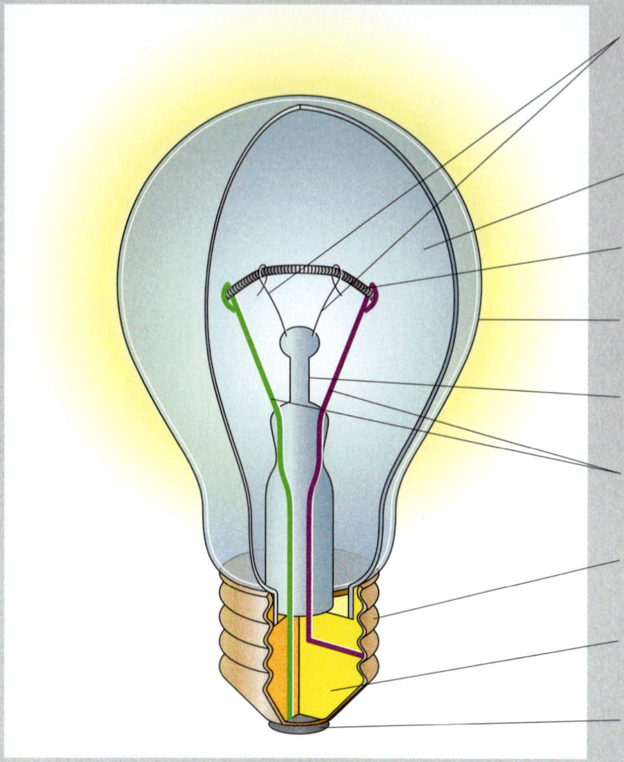

1 ______
2 ______
3 ______
4 ______
5 ______
6 ______
7 outer ______
8 ______
9 inner ______

At its base, an incandescent light bulb has two metal contacts, an outer screw thread contact (*Schraubsockel*) and an inner electrical foot contact (*Kontaktplättchen*), isolated from each other by insulation. The metal contacts connect with two wire conductors (*Zuleitungsdrähte*) that carry current to and from the tungsten filament (*Glühdraht*). The filament is held in place by two support wires (*Haltedrähte*) joined to a vertical glass mount (*Glasträger*). The whole device is housed in a sealed glass bulb (*Glaskolben*) filled with an inert gas (*Edelgas*), generally argon

3 Main Course
Media madness

1 MODAL VERBS

›› SB page 64, Grammar checkpoint

A Complete part of the conversation between Debbie, Claire, Dave and Steve on their way to the cinema. Use these forms. Sometimes more than one answer is possible.

can | can't | could | should | shouldn't | ought to

Steve: Well, which film are we going to go to?

Dave: I don't have any strong feelings, but what about the sci-fi movie? I don't know anything about it, but it ____________[1] be quite good. What do you think, Debbie?

Debbie: Well, OK, if that's what you really want …

Claire: Well, it isn't what I want! I haven't had anything to eat since breakfast and I'm really hungry. I ____________[2] eat something before I do anything else. But *Journey to the Stars* starts at 6.30, so we ____________[3] go to a restaurant first if we go to that one.

Steve: Right. Let's forget *Journey to the Stars*. Listen, we ____________[4] go to the new *Pirates of the Caribbean*. It's great!

Claire: Oh, no! We definitely ____________[5] go to that. It's so silly! Let's go to *One Night in New York* instead. It's on at 8.30, so we ____________[6] have something to eat before it starts.

B Complete the next part of the conversation. Use each of these forms twice.

must | mustn't | needn't

Steve: OK, then. Let's go to a restaurant first and then to *One Night in New York*. Personally, I ____________[1] get home by any special time.
The only thing is this: I ____________[2] call my parents if we are going to be late.

Claire: I ____________[3] call my parents because they never worry. But I ____________[4] be home later than 11.30.

Dave: I don't have any choice. It's about the car. I ____________[5] get home late with it, or Dad won't let me borrow it again.

Debbie: And I really ____________[6] be home early because I have an important test at school tomorrow. I need my sleep!

C Now write three sentences of your own to show that you understand the difference between *must*, *mustn't* and *needn't*.

____

____

____

2 MODAL VERB SUBSTITUTES

›› SB page 64, Grammar checkpoint

A Match the modal substitutes a–d to the modal verbs 1–4.

1	d	**can/cannot:** for ability & possibility	a	do not have to
2		**can/cannot** for permission	b	have to
3		**must** for necessity	c	(not) be allowed to
4		**needn't** for non-necessity	d	(not) be able to

B Complete the sentences with appropriate modal substitutes in the correct past form.

With all his equipment in the back of the Landrover, cameraman Rob Green arrived early at the Chakragar Nature Reserve, ready for work. However, for several hours, he had to [1] (*müssen*) wait at the entrance. He ________ [2] (*nicht dürfen*) enter because he needed a special licence to film there. There was no alternative: he ________ [3] (*müssen*) wait until the special permission arrived. At 4 p.m., the guards finally received permission to let him film in the Reserve for a week, and so he ________ [4] (*dürfen*) enter. But because it was late in the day, he ________ [5] (*nicht können*) start work that day, and he ________ [6] (*müssen*) find a place to camp instead. At last, early next morning, Rob ________ [7] (*können*) start work. He climbed and climbed and finally found the perfect place to hide with his cameras. He ________ [8] (*nicht müssen*) wait long before the first animals arrived ...

C Now complete the sentences with appropriate modal substitutes in the correct past or *will* future forms.

His aim was to film the rare snow leopard in the wild, and this was not an easy thing to do. For the next six days, he got wonderful pictures of other animals and birds, but he ________ [1] (*nicht können*) get the pictures that he wanted. He was very worried because by this time he was thinking, 'My one-week licence means that they won't let me stay any longer, and I ________ [2] (*nicht dürfen*) do any more filming. So I ________ [3] (*müssen*) go home tomorrow without any film of the leopards.' But just then, his luck changed. A leopard appeared and started chasing a deer from rock to rock down a steep cliff. Rob ________ [4] (*nicht müssen*) do anything except turn on his camera, and he ________ [5] (*können*) catch the whole dramatic scene on film! In the voiceover which he later added to his documentary *A Week in Chakragar*, he said, 'In a few years from now, I believe that we ________ [6] (*nicht können*) find anything like this any more. And to see one of these amazing animals, we ________ [7] (*müssen*) go to a zoo. Sadly, there will be none left in the wild. Not one.'

3 PROBLEMS WITH MODAL VERBS

›› SB page 64, Grammar checkpoint

Cross out the mistake in each sentence and write the correct word(s).

1 She ~~can~~ French better than Italian. *can speak*

2 We mustn't go shopping. We have everything we need. ____________

3 Last week, I must fly to New York. ____________

4 Do you can understand this book? ____________

5 You don't mustn't talk like that. It's rude ____________

6 He can't decide. He doesn't know what he will. ____________

7 I'm going to tell the assistant I would the blue coat, not the green one. ____________

4 BUILDING SKILLS: MEDIATION

›› SB page 62, exercise 6

You have a German friend who wants to join an English-language forum that discusses media news. His English is quite good, but you know that he likes to express his opinions very strongly.

You think the information on Netiquette (page 62 in your Student's Book) could help your friend. Translate paragraph 2 and the six rules to email to him.

____

____

____

____

____

____

____

____

____

5 WORDFIELD: THE MEDIA

A Find 18 words in the word square.

X	C	E	L	E	B	R	I	T	Y	T	Z	T	E	X	T	I	N	G	R	P	U	P	I	K
V	W	Q	A	J	K	L	Y	X	E	F	R	Q	A	W	E	S	R	D	C	R	V	R	N	P
I	G	P	O	P	U	L	A	R	I	G	E	M	V	I	E	W	E	R	B	E	D	O	F	R
T	M	D	S	B	M	P	L	W	L	R	A	P	L	O	K	I	J	N	M	S	U	G	H	O
I	N	T	E	R	A	C	T	I	V	E	L	R	C	O	M	E	D	Y	E	S	X	R	C	D
E	D	R	F	V	B	G	T	Z	H	N	I	U	J	I	M	O	P	Y	A	W	Q	A	E	U
Q	Y	M	O	B	I	L	E	E	S	D	T	R	T	O	F	F	L	I	N	E	U	M	F	C
M	N	B	G	V	F	V	F	E	D	C	Y	E	M	X	D	E	W	S	A	Q	I	M	D	E
D	E	D	A	U	D	I	E	N	C	E	V	R	O	M	E	S	S	A	G	E	K	E	D	R
R	F	V	B	C	D	E	S	W	X	M	U	J	V	Z	H	N	B	R	F	W	B	L	O	G
E	N	T	E	R	T	A	I	N	I	N	G	R	I	W	P	U	I	B	G	V	R	C	E	W
G	C	H	R	J	I	C	E	U	T	Z	B	Q	E	D	O	C	U	M	E	N	T	A	R	Y

B Now complete the following sentences with words from the word square.

1 *Big Brother* is an example of the sort of ____________________ TV that has become very common.

2 ____________________ is cheaper than making an ordinary phone call.

3 Some shows can attract an ____________________ of several million.

4 For TV advertisers, each ____________________ is a possible customer.

5 The TV review says the film is a ____________________ , but I didn't think it was very funny!

6 As people get more and more news online and from TV, it seems that the ____________________ is slowly losing readers.

7 Jessica went to India for 6 months but she kept us informed of what she was doing through a ____________________ on the internet.

6 *A Week in Chakragar* is a ____________________ about snow leopards.

6 TECHNICAL OPTIONS

›› SB page 63

Complete the description of the front panel of a typical DVD player with terms from the drawing.

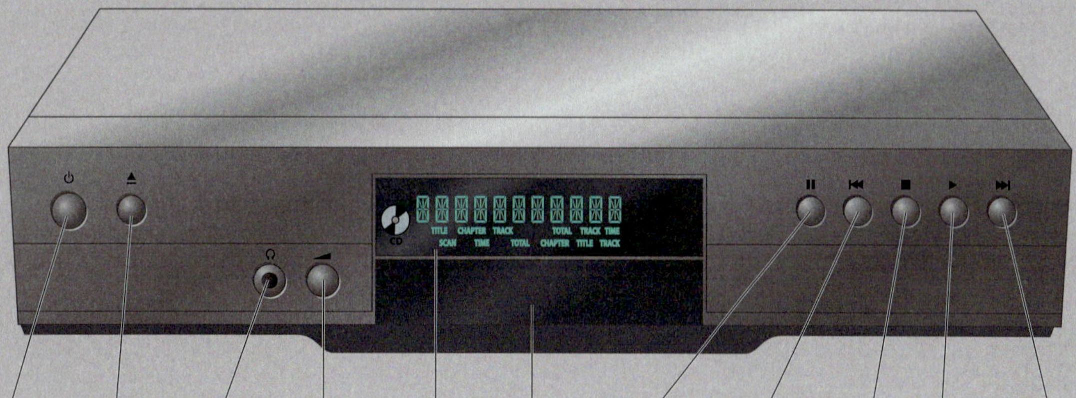

Let's look at the *front panel* [1] of the player first. The ____________________ [2] switch is located top left with the ____________________ [3] button for the disc tray to the right of it. Below these two controls to the right there is a jack socket for ____________________ [4] with the ____________________ [5] control next to it.

The ____________________ [6] is situated in the middle of the front panel with the ____________________ [7] immediately below it. The display shows the DVD title, the ____________________ [8] now playing and the ____________________ [9] so far.

The five standard DVD control buttons, i. e. ____________________ [10], chapter skip backwards, ____________________ [11], play and ____________________ [12] forwards are located top right.

4 Main Course
On the move

1 *IF*-SENTENCES TYPE 1

›› SB page 74, Grammar checkpoint

Steve and Carrie are out on their new bikes and are choosing a route. Use the ideas in the picture to write their conversation.

1 **Steve:** Listen. If we go west, we'll get to Dustville. And if we go there, we'll be able to go to the concert in the park.

Carrie: Yes, but we'll have to ride through the noisy, dirty city if we do that.

2 **Carrie:** Now look, if we go north, we'll get up ______________________.

And if we go there, we'll ______________________.

Steve: Yes, but we'll ______________________.

3 **Steve:** What about this idea? If we ______________________

______________________.

Carrie: Yes, but ______________________.

4 **Carrie:** What about another idea? If ______________________

______________________.

Steve: ______________________.

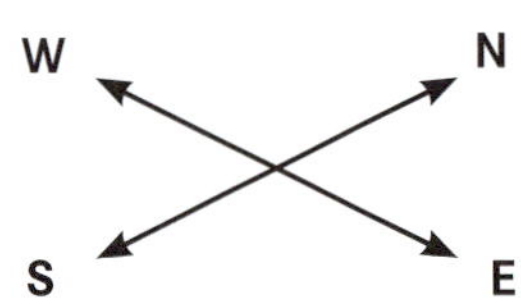

get to Dustville
for: be able to go to the concert in the park
against: have to ride through the noisy, dirty city

get up into the mountains
for: have some beautiful views
against: have to climb lots of steep hills

get into the forest
for: can have a picnic by the river
against: might get lost in the forest

get down to the beach
for: be able to go for a swim
against: get sand in all our clothes

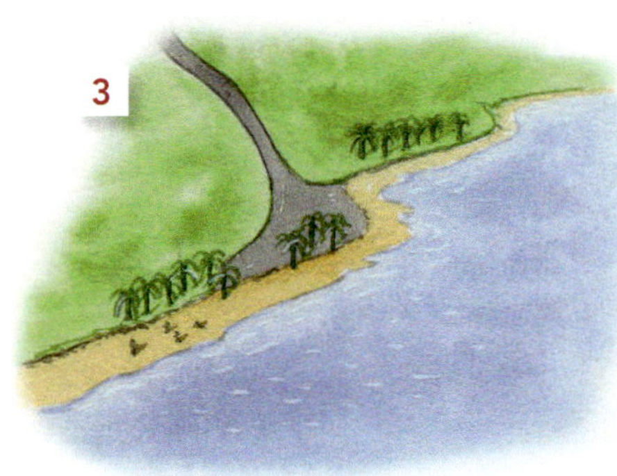

2 *IF*-SENTENCES TYPE 2

›› SB page 74, Grammar checkpoint

Imagine that you are now on your bike at the crossroads instead of Steve and Carrie. Answer these questions with *if*-sentences type 2.

1 You are hot and want to go swimming. Which way would you go?

If I was hot and ______, I would ______

______

2 Your gears (= *Gangschaltung*) are broken. Where would you go to find a bike shop?

If my ______

______

3 You want some photos of beautiful views across the country. Which way would you go?

______

______

4 You are tired and want to have a sleep somewhere cool and quiet. Where would you go?

______

______

3 *IF*-SENTENCES TYPES 1 AND 2

›› SB page 74, Grammar checkpoint

Read the situations. Then use the sentence parts to form *if*-sentences, types 1 or 2, as appropriate.

1 You and your friend have to catch a bus in five minutes, but he is still getting ready to go out. You say to him: we (miss) / bus / you (not hurry)

We'll miss the bus if you don't hurry.

2 However, your friend knows that there are lots of buses. He says: / we (miss) that bus, another one (soon come) and we (be able) / catch that.

______

______

3 Julie and Pete live and work in different cities. They cannot leave their jobs, and it is difficult for them to meet. Julie writes to him: / one of us (move), we (can be) together all the time

______

______

4 Pete has very little money at the moment. He writes back: / I (have) enough money, I (buy) / car, and then I (be able) / visit / more often.

______

______

5 Your friend is trying to choose between two cars. One is smaller and has a smaller engine. The other one is bigger and more powerful. You say to her: you (save) money on petrol / you (choose) / smaller one

______

______

6 You know that smaller cars are better for the environment, but you also know that a lot of people prefer faster, more powerful vehicles. You say: / everybody (buy) smaller cars, it (be) better for / environment

______

______

4 WORD FAMILIES

›› SB page 66, text

A Complete the table with words from Section A text lines 1–27 and words that you know or can work out. (Check your dictionary if necessary.)

Verb	Noun	Adjective *-ing* form	Adjective *-ed* form
pollute		polluting	
damage			damaged
		exhausting	exhausted
	improvement	improving	
	increase		increased

B Use words from A to complete the following.

1 *Increasing* levels of income in countries like China and India are leading to huge *increases* in the numbers of cars.

2 We live in an increasingly ____________[1] environment, and we human beings are probably the ones that are causing most of the ____________[2] .

3 To reduce ____________[1] , we have to get older, more ____________[2] vehicles off the roads.

4 Many local governments are ____________[1] their public transport systems. This means fewer cars on the roads and big ____________[2] in emission levels.

5 However, public transport is not perfect. Travel on Tokyo's over-crowded trains is ____________[1] , and in the evening millions of ____________[2] passengers fall asleep on their long journeys home.

5 WORDFIELD: TRANSPORT

Do the tree puzzle. Complete 1–9 to find and write out 10.

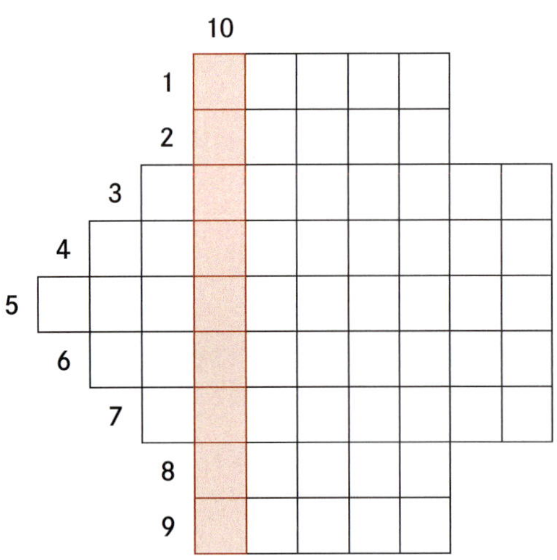

1 The government gets a lot of money from car drivers from fuel and vehicle ... .
2 Shall we take the ... through the mountains or the one along the coast?
3 In the rush hour every morning there is a three-kilometre ... along this road.
4 There wasn't much traffic on the new road at first, but quite soon it was just as ... as the old one.
5 These trains now carry 1,000 ... across the country at 300kph.
6 Prices have gone up again. Petrol is now more ... than it has ever been before.
7 Tony is a long-distance ... . He travels for three hours a day to and from work.
8 The new electric vehicles have an improved ... of up to 280 kilometres.
9 Goods leave the factory by ... and travel by road to our customers up and down the country.

10 The missing word is: ____________ .

6 BUILDING SKILLS: DESCRIBING AND COMMENTING ON CARTOONS

›› SB page 68, exercise 4

A First label the sentence parts in order 1–6.

B Then label each D, A or C according to the D-A-C method: D for Describing; A for Analyzing; C for Commenting on the cartoon.

		it also shows/passengers/helpless/ and cannot/
		however/my opinion/not fair/attack German trains/this way since/
1	D	cartoon shows/station/lot/passengers who/waiting/
		cartoon suggests/trains/often late/ unreliable
		cartoonist may be right/trains in Britain/ America
		near us, we/see/female passenger who looks* ... and ... as she reads/sign which directs her to/

* (See the list of adjectives on page 65 of your Student's Book.)

C Now expand the sentences to write an analysis of the cartoon in your exercise book.

This cartoon shows a station with a lot of passengers who are waiting for a ...

7 TECHNICAL OPTIONS

›› SB page 73

Label the outline of the car with words/expressions from the box.

aerial | bonnet | bumper | driver's door | front grill | headlight | numberplate | rear light | roof | side window | tyre | wheel | windscreen | wing | wing mirror

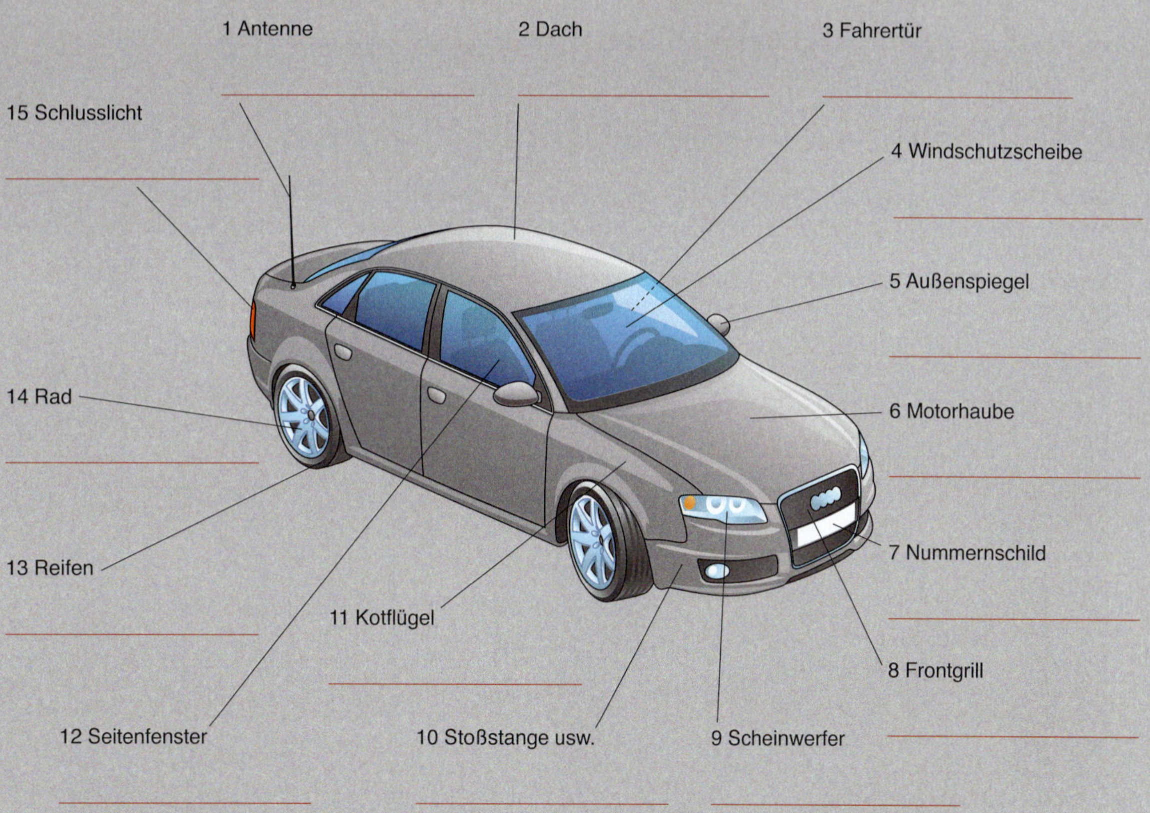

5

Main Course

Green enough?

1 WORD PAIRS

›› SB page 80, text

A Use words from the box to form important word pairs from the text.

change | emissions | fuels | fusion | levels | power | Revolution | warming

1 Industrial ______________________
2 climate ______________________
3 sea ______________________
4 fossil ______________________
5 CO_2 ______________________
6 solar ______________________
7 nuclear ______________________
8 global ______________________

B Use word pairs from A to complete the following.

1 People are beginning to leave low-lying islands because of rising ______________________ .
2 With an average 1 °C temperature rise in the last century, ______________________ seems to be real.
3 The ______________________ began with the start of new factories in places like Manchester nearly three centuries ago.
4 For Europe, ______________________ may mean hotter summers but also wetter winters.
5 Most scientists now agree that ______________________ from human sources such as cars are helping to raise temperatures worldwide.
6 Earth receives huge amounts of energy from the sun, and many people believe that we should use this ______________________ much more than we do.
7 Most environmental problems come from our use of ______________________ – coal, gas and oil.
8 ______________________ may one day give us all the cheap, safe, clean power that we want. and so we will no longer need any of today's energy sources.

2 PAST PERFECT

›› SB page 84, Grammar checkpoint

Read the monologue from the start of another disaster movie, *When the Aliens Came*. Put the verbs in the simple past or past perfect, as appropriate. Use the past perfect when both tenses are possible.

At first, as I slowly woke up *woke up* , (wake up), I *did not know* (not know) how long I *had lain* (lie) there in that cave high in the mountains. However, I soon ______________[1] (realize) that I ______________[2] (be) there for many hours. I ______________[3] (arrive) there in the heat of the morning, but looking out, I ______________[4] (see) the last of the evening sun. I ______________[5] (think) about the people that I ______________[6] (leave) in the burning city that morning. Perhaps the aliens ____________________ [7] (kill) them all already. I ____________________ [8] (try) to stand up, but pain ____________________ [9] (shoot) through my leg. I ____________________ [10] (remember) that I ____________________ [11] (fall) badly on my way up the mountain side. Perhaps I ____________________ [12] (break) a bone! Suddenly, I ____________________ [13] (freeze) in horror: a shadow ____________________ [14] (fall) over the mouth of the cave. Then I ____________________ [15] (hear) the low humming noise that I ____________________ [16] (learn) to fear the previous night when the alien spaceships ____________________ [17] (start) to attack the city. Clearly, the aliens ____________________ [18] (find out) about my escape somehow, and one of their deadly spacecraft ____________________ [19] (follow) my path to the secret cave.

3 *IF*-SENTENCES TYPE 3

›› SB page 84, Grammar checkpoint

Use the pictures and sentence parts to write about a long-distance drive that went very wrong. Use *if*-sentences type 3. Start like this:

1 not wake up late / get up on time

If Mark hadn't woken up late, he would have ____________________

____________________.

2 have time to plan / trip

If he'd got up ____________________

____________________.

3 remember / check / water

____

____________________.

4 car not break down

____

____________________.

5 not have to push / for hours

____

____________________.

6 not miss / party

____

____________________.

4 BUILDING SKILLS: SUMMARIZING

›› SB page 82, exercise 4

The following sentences are mixed-up summaries of two of the films in Focus on page 75.

A Find the sentences that belong to each summary.
(Use reference words, e.g. pronouns, to help order the sentences.)
B Write out the complete summaries.
C Add the film title to each paragraph.

The story follows them through to the explosion at the last possible moment.

As it opens, we meet the Mariner (Kevin Costner), who sails the ocean alone, always searching for fresh water.

From this, we move to NASA's discovery that it is going to happen again.

This movie is set in a post-apocalyptic future world where most land is now underwater.

Attacking the three of them time after time are the evil 'smokers'.

He soon finds himself unhappily giving protection to Helen and the child Enola.

These Hell's Angels on water burn oil, smoke and generally behave badly towards everyone else.

This movie is set in the days before a huge asteroid is due to hit Earth.

To do this, Stamper has to die, but the asteroid is destroyed and Earth is saved.

This small girl unknowingly carries the secret of the route to dry land in the form of a map on her back.

The only people who can drill the necessary hole are a wild group of oil drillers led by Harry Stamper (Bruce Willis).

It opens with the information that it happened 65 million years ago and could happen again.

After many dangers, the smokers are destroyed, and the heroes find the paradise of dry land.

The only answer is a nuclear explosion deep inside the asteroid to blow it to pieces.

Title: ______________________

This movie is set in a post-apocalyptic future world where most land is now underwater.
As it opens, ______________________

____

Title: ______________________

____

5 WORDFIELD: THE ENVIRONMENT

Do the crossword puzzle.

Across

1 a situation where all systems have collapsed
3 the type of weather that an area has
4 a fuel that is not solid like coal or liquid like oil
6 Water becomes this at 0 °C.
8 energy that we need e. g. for heating, lighting and making machines work
10 to do with the regular rise and fall of the sea
12 colour; here connected with looking after the environment
13 act of joining together
14 person, place or thing that provides something that we need, e. g. energy

Down

2 the air around the Earth (or another planet)
5 to stay away from something, to prevent something from happening
7 the area of land along the edge of the sea
9 a large area of land with geographical, cultural or political differences from other areas
11 a measure of weight equal to 1,000 kilograms

6 TECHNICAL OPTIONS

›› SB page 83

Look at the graph and say if the statements are true (T) or false (F). Correct the four false statements (in your exercise book).

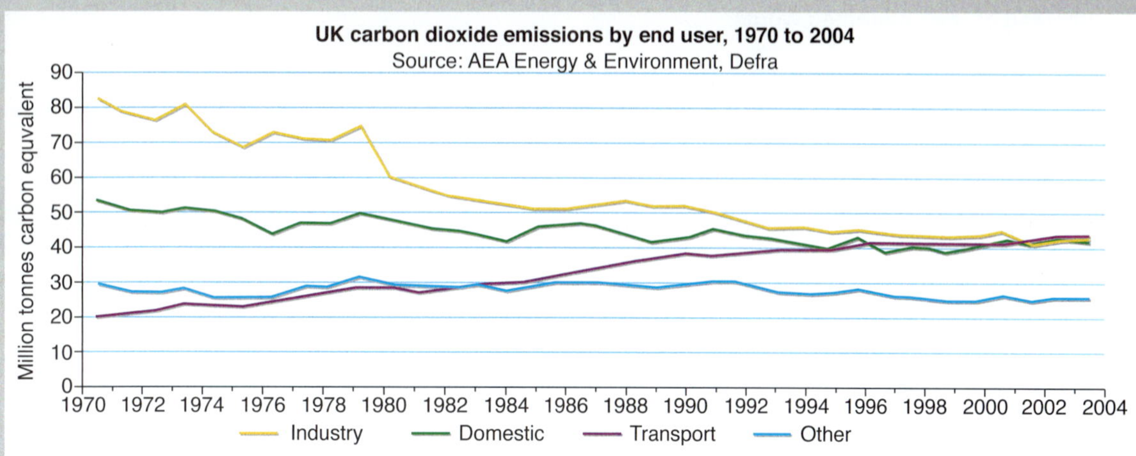

*domestic = *Haushalts-*

	True	False
1 The graph shows CO_2 emissions in the UK from 1970 to 2004.	☐	☐
2 The graph focuses on three main sources of CO_2 emissions.	☐	☐
3 In 1970, industry produced most CO_2, followed by transport.	☐	☐
4 In 1996, transport and domestic users produced roughly equal amounts of CO_2.	☐	☐
5 During the period as a whole, industrial emissions almost halved.	☐	☐
6 Domestic emissions have dropped from just over 60 million tonnes to just over 50 million.	☐	☐
7 The biggest increase in emissions was in transport.	☐	☐
8 Emission from other sources have also increased sharply.	☐	☐

Modern ways to work

1 VOCABULARY

›› SB page 85, Focus

A Complete the sentences with words from the boxes. Then add the correct job title from Focus activity 1.

challenging | customer contact | independent | regular hours | repetitive | responsible

Job title: ______________________

I like working with people and so my present job with lots of ______________________[1] is just right for me. I also like it because it's not ______________________[2]: every day is different – even though I only have to work the same ______________________[3] as the sales staff. And sometimes the problems that I have to solve are quite difficult and ______________________[4]. I have to think for myself and be quite ______________________[5]. There's nobody else to ask. It's a ______________________[6] job, too, as the company must keep people happy.

B Rewrite the sentences using the words in brackets (all from pages 85–86 in your Student's Book) instead of the underlined words.

1 I'm <u>training to be a secretary</u>. (secretarial course)

____

2 I've just <u>qualified</u> in business studies. (qualification)

____

3 I <u>sent out</u> lots of <u>applications</u> for different jobs. (apply)

____

4 <u>Friendliness</u> is an important part of the work. (friendly)

____

5 I have to do everything <u>with great accuracy</u>. (accurately)

____

6 <u>The complexity of</u> today's world of work is amazing. (complex)

____

7 My new job <u>challenges me a lot</u> in many different ways. (challenging)

____

8 <u>There is more flexibility in the area of</u> training now than there used to be. (flexible)

____

2 BUILDING SKILLS: TAKING NOTES FROM READING

›› SB page 87, exercise 2

Ed Fisher has got an interview with BSG Solar. Before his interview, Ed wants to find out about the company. Read the newspaper article and complete Ed's notes.

BSG Solar: 21 Today

BSG Solar celebrates its 21st birthday this week, and looks back on a big journey from very small beginnings.

As founder and Director of this private, family-owned firm, Barry S Good says, 'We're growing rapidly, and our story shows that it is possible to turn today's environmental worries into a real business success story.' The firm specializes in supplying and fitting solar heating systems, a popular answer to the problem of rising energy costs.

The proof of BSG Solar's success is in the figures. The company now employs 550 people in 57 centres across the south of England. This is a long way from the early days when Barry first opened as BSG Heating in Oxford with just three employees. In those days, the young business supplied and fitted traditional gas central heating systems.

BSG Solar's Head Office is in the building where Barry began. Then, it contained a workshop, a store for equipment and just a small office. Now, though, the same space contains nothing but the offices that are necessary to provide the central services that are necessary for the growing organization.

BSG SOLAR **General:**

Type of organization: ______________ Director: ______________

Head Office in: ______________ Founded: ______________

Changes:	21 years ago	Now
Staff:	______________	______________
Centres:	______________	______________
The Oxford centre:	______________	______________
Type of business:	______________	______________

3 PRESENT PERFECT PROGRESSIVE AND PRESENT PERFECT

›› SB page 94, Grammar checkpoint

Complete BSG Solar's website. Where both tenses are possible, use the present perfect progressive.

Home | News | Links | Help

BSG Solar can look back on a big success story. Here are just a few of the high points.

- The company *has just opened* [1] (just open) a new centre in south-east London – its fifth in London and 57th across the country.
- With today's continuing energy problems, the organization *has been growing* [2] (grow) especially rapidly in the last three years.
- The company ______________ [3] (supply) heating systems across the whole country since 2005.
- This year, we ______________ [4] (become) the UK's largest solar heating supplier.
- And as of today, we ______________ [5] (fit) a total of 27,573 systems.
- Not only this, but BSG Solar ______________ [6] (also win) several important industry prizes and awards in recent years.
- Recently, the company ______________ [7] (upgrade) its IT and other systems at Head Office in Oxford in order to keep up with its rapid growth.
- With this in mind, we ______________ [8] (look for) enthusiastic new members of staff to work in our IT and Finance Departments.

4 SIMPLE PAST AND PRESENT PERFECT

›› SB page 94, Grammar checkpoint

Complete part of Ed's interview with Barry Good at BSG Solar. Put the verbs in the simple past or present perfect.

Barry: Now, you *'ve been* ¹ (be) on an IT course over at the CFE since last year, *haven't* ² you?

Ed: That's right, Mr Good, and I ______ ³ (just/finish). I ______ ⁴ (take) my last exam yesterday.

Barry: Oh, right. ______ they ______ ⁵ (give) you your results yet?

Ed: No, not yet. But I ______ ⁶ (have) good grades for my course work through the year,so I think I ______ ⁷ (pass).

Barry: But you ______ ⁸ (start) at the CFE the September before last, ______ ⁹ you? ______ you ______ ¹⁰ (do) an IT course in your first year, too?

Ed: No, I ______ ¹¹ (be) on an access programme to improve my general education before I ______ ¹² (begin) the diploma course.

Barry: So you ______ ¹³ (put) yourself through two years of education as an adult, ______ ¹⁴ you?

Ed: Yes, that's right, Mr Good.

Barry: Well, I think that shows real commitment, and that's something I like to see in people who work for me!

5 WORDFIELD: WORK

Find 18 words in the words square.

Q	T	E	M	P	O	R	A	R	Y	P	S	C	T	E	C	H	N	I	C	I	A	N	X	A
R	W	E	D	C	X	S	W	A	C	L	A	A	S	D	B	N	Y	I	K	N	F	P	M	R
E	C	O	N	T	R	A	C	T	L	Q	L	Z	E	X	P	E	R	I	E	N	C	E	B	O
C	E	R	X	H	V	C	D	B	E	Y	E	Q	S	X	C	D	E	R	F	V	T	G	X	U
E	Z	E	Q	T	I	O	Z	V	R	B	S	P	R	O	D	U	C	T	I	O	N	H	Q	T
P	Y	M	S	E	T	M	N	M	K	A	P	T	E	D	L	M	N	T	Z	U	I	R	E	I
T	T	P	T	F	Z	M	U	B	S	R	E	T	W	O	R	K	P	L	A	C	E	F	E	N
I	F	L	G	A	H	I	J	E	X	F	R	D	W	E	F	T	G	Z	H	U	J	I	C	E
O	V	O	B	C	N	T	M	N	E	T	S	C	W	D	P	R	O	S	P	E	C	T	S	M
N	C	Y	Z	T	M	M	I	E	D	G	O	V	V	F	R	T	G	B	Z	H	N	Z	H	N
I	X	E	H	O	J	E	K	F	C	B	N	F	Z	I	N	T	E	R	V	I	E	W	D	C
S	Y	R	J	R	U	N	O	I	W	A	I	T	E	R	M	N	B	G	F	V	D	C	S	X
T	Q	E	M	Y	I	T	L	T	R	U	Z	U	H	N	E	M	P	L	O	Y	M	E	N	T

6 PROBLEMS WITH VERBS

Cross out the mistake in each sentence and write the correct word(s).

1 Ben ~~is taking~~ the train to college every morning. *takes*

2 Terry and Julia can't go out. They do their homework. ______

3 I am liking my new job more and more. ______

4 Tom didn't start college on Day 1. He travelled back from India at the time. ______

5 Annie will have a baby, so she's taking maternity leave. ______

6 Kirsty and James work here for two years. ______

7 I'm sorry, but the manager isn't here. She just go home. ______

8 Tony and Emma have been knowing each other since they did Business Studies together. ______

9 The computer doesn't start! What's wrong with it? ______

10 I would accept the job if they would offer it to me. ______

7 TECHNICAL OPTIONS

›› SB page 93

A Ask and answer wh-questions about the accident.

1 who/work/scaffold/time/accident/?

Who was working on the scaffold at the time of the accident?

Barry Sands and Len Moore.

2 what/men + do/when/accident/happen?

What ______

They ______

3 where/accident/take place?

______

______

4 why/scaffold/lean over/sharp angle?

______

______

5 why/Barry/fall/scaffold/?

______

______

B Find words or expressions to fit the definitions.

1 safety device to stop user falling from a height ______

2 safety device to protect user's head ______

3 movable equipment to enable user to work at a height ______

4 surveillance device used to record what is happening ______

5 vehicle for delivering concrete to construction sites ______

6 vehicle for transporting sick and/or injured people ______

Main Course

7 Going global

1 VOCABULARY

›› SB page 96, text; page 99, text

**A Complete Table 1 with words from the Section A text.
Complete Table 2 with words from the Section B text.**

1

Verb	Noun
globalize	________
solve	________
transmit	________
________	development
________	requirement
employ	________

2

Noun	Adjective
________	free
________	redundant
________	strong
________	weak
independence	________
competition	________

B Look at the highlighted words. Use related words from A to help rewrite the sentences.

1 With its name for reliability, the Black Cat brand has real strength.
With its name for reliability, the Black Cat brand is ____________________.

2 During the last 50 years, there has been a rapid development in free trade.
During the last 50 years, free trade ____________________.

3 It's the technicians' job to find a solution to the problem.
It's the technicians' job to ____________________.

4 Many workers have no freedom to ask for better conditions.
Many workers ____________________.

5 These days, it costs very little to transmit data electronically.
These days, electronic ____________________.

2 WORDFIELD: GLOBALIZATION

Do the tree puzzle. Complete 1–9 to find and write out 10.

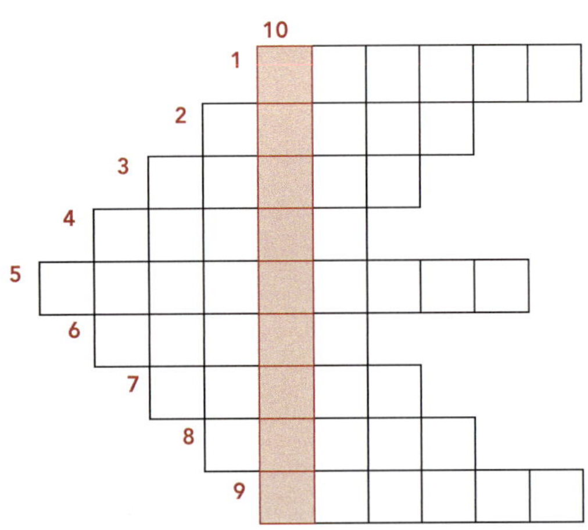

1 money that is made from selling – after paying all business costs
2 summer food from trees that is often transported round the world to be sold somewhere else in winter
3 things that are produced for sale
4 the activities of buying and selling goods or services
5 people who buy and use goods and services
6 the amount of money you have to pay to buy something
7 describing something that is lower in price than you expect
8 a product or group of products with its own name
9 an amount of something that is available to be used

10 ____________________

3 BUILDING SKILLS: WRITING A COMMENT

›› SB page 102, exercise 4

A Choose the correct connectors to complete the comment.

Comment on the following: 'People's jobs are more important than cheap goods in the shops.'

This view suggests that we should keep out cheap goods from places like China in order to protect our own industries and jobs. Because/While [1] some people strongly support this view, others are strongly against it. Let us consider some of the arguments for and against the protectionist view. On the one hand,/For example, [2] the loss of jobs causes great personal problems and huge social pressures. In addition,/On the other hand, [3] lack of competition lets protected local producers refuse to develop better products at lower prices. As a result,/Despite this, [4] the local economy slowly gets weaker and people get poorer.

Moreover,/Therefore, [5] it is clear that there is no easy choice to make. For instance,/However, [6] it seems to me that ______________________________ .

My main reason for saying this is that ______________________________

____

B Now add your own views in the paragraph above.

4 THE PASSIVE: DESCRIBING A PROCESS

›› SB page 104, Grammar checkpoint

Use the sentence parts to describe the car production process.

1 all/car parts (deliver)/factory just/time for use

All the car parts are delivered to the factory just in

____

2 /parts (take) straight to/production line

____

____

3 /body (put together) separately from/rest of/car

____

____

4 then/engine and all/other parts (mount) in/body

____

____

5 at/end, everything (check) very carefully/quality controllers

____

____

6 finally,/finished cars (load) onto transporters and (distribute) all over/world

____

____

5 THE PASSIVE: QUESTIONS

›› SB page 104, Grammar checkpoint

Jack emailed his new boss Margaret Beckwith about 'Baskets of Bengal' (Grammar checkpoint, Exercise 2). Margaret has some questions. Write her email back. Put her questions in the passive.

Jack:

Re: Baskets of Bengal

Just a few questions if I may.

1 *Will Stephen Carter's travel costs be paid by B of B?*
2 ______
3 ______
4 ______
5 ______
6 ______
7 ______

6 PASSIVE WITH MODALS

›› SB page 104, Grammar checkpoint

Write Jack's reply to Margaret. Use his answers and modals in the passive.

Margaret:

In answer to your questions:

1 (Yes / have to) *Yes, Stephen Carter's travel costs have to be paid by B by B.*
2 (No / should / soon) ______
3 (1,000 / ought to) ______
4 (No / needn't) ______
5 (Yes / could) ______
6 (All shops / might) ______
7 (Yes / have to) ______

7 PROBLEMS WITH PASSIVES

›› SB page 104, Grammar checkpoint

Cross out the mistake in each sentence and write the correct word(s). (In one sentence, no words are needed.)

1 With all the new orders, extra production was requiring at the second factory. ____________

2 Bill has just offered a new job in export sales. ____________

3 Our Kenyan FAIRTRADE coffee can bought at any of our stores. ____________

4 More information about FairTrade may be found on the website by you. ____________

5 I hope the people who treat their workers so badly will be catched and punished. ____________

6 This interesting new book, *Globally Speaking*, is from the famous Dr James Ronson. ____________

7 These beautiful FAIRTRADE shirts are made from pure cotton. ____________

8 It said that the Chinese economy will one day be larger than America's. ____________

8 TECHNICAL OPTIONS

›› SB page 103

Match a sentence part from list A to one from list B to make true statements about the Øresund Link.

A		B
1 The Link provides a short route	☐	a about 13000 vehicles to use it every day.
2 Today, Mark Sutton is reporting live	☐	b to the Swedish mainland near Malmö.
3 The Link is made up of four sections,	☐	c between Sweden and Denmark without taking a ferry.
4 The tunnel joins the Kastrup peninsula in Denmark	☐	d for road vehicles and a lower one for trains.
5 The Link has two decks, an upper deck	☐	e from the island of Satholm in the Baltic Sea.
6 The suspension bridge itself connects Peberholm	☐	f the highest part of the bridge are 204 metres tall.
7 The two pylons that support	☐	g to the artificial island of Peberholm.
8 The company that runs the Link expects	☐	h including a 4-kilometre-long road and rail tunnel.

8 Finding a job in the EU

1 VOCABULARY

›› SB page 106, texts

Use one of the phrases from the box to complete the sentences.

are not paid | can make a contribution | chooses the UK | do a period | does not give the name | emails Lisa the name | is studying tourism | pay a fee to get | require students | SEC specializes in

1 Lisa ______________________________ at a university in Bremen.
2 Students have to ______________________________ of practical training abroad.
3 Some courses ______________________________ to go to an English-speaking country.
4 Lisa ______________________________ because it is similar to Germany.
5 The online agency ______________________________ arranging internships abroad.
6 SEC's ad ______________________________ of the host company.
7 Unfortunately, interns ______________________________ a salary.
8 The host company ______________________________ towards an intern's living expenses.
9 Lisa has to ______________________________ full details of the internship.
10 SEC ______________________________ of a contact person in Norwich.

2 BUILDING SKILLS: WRITING A CV

›› SB page 108, exercises 3–6

1 Use numbers from 1 to 6 to put Tobias Kraft's personal details into the correct order. Put a cross (X) by the two items they do not belong in this section of a CV at all.

2 Tick (✓) the items you would expect to find in the Interests and skills section of a CV, and cross (x) the items that do not belong there.

TOBIAS KRAFT

Personal details

- ☐ Daytime phone number
- ☐ Address
- ☐ Marital status
- ☐ Date and place of birth
- ☐ Email address
- ☐ Sex
- ☐ Name
- ☐ Nationality

TOBIAS KRAFT

Interests and skills

- ☐ References
- ☐ Cycling and camping
- ☐ English and Spanish
- ☐ LAN parties
- ☐ EU class C driving licence
- ☐ Martin-Luther-Grundschule
- ☐ Member Red Cross
- ☐ MS Office

3 GERUND OR INFINITIVE?

›› SB page 114, Grammar checkpoint

A Complete the table with verbs from the box.

admit | afford | ~~begin~~ | continue | deny | dislike | ~~dream of~~ | enjoy | expect | finish | hate | hope | imagine | intend | like | love | mention | practise | prefer | promise | start | stop *(unterbrechen)* | want | ~~would prefer~~

Infinitive	Gerund	Both
would prefer	*dream of*	*begin*

B Use a verb or verb form from the table + infinitive or gerund to express the ideas below. Sie möchten jemandem sagen, dass Sie …

1 … versprochen haben, rechtzeitig anzukommen.

____

2 … immer davon geträumt haben, im Ausland zu arbeiten.

____

3 … sich nicht vorstellen können, viel Geld zu gewinnen.

____

4 … es Freitagabend vorziehen würden, zu Hause zu bleiben.

____

5 … begonnen haben, Französisch zu lernen.

____

6 … anhalten müssen, um Geld zu holen.

____

4 VOCABULARY

›› SB page 112, exercise 2

Cross out the incorrect form.

1 Nowadays, most EU states recommend / ~~recommended~~ [1] that children are educated in mix / mixed [2] classes.

2 The EU is threatened / threatening [1] to break off negotiations with Romania if the country doesn't fight corrupt / corruption [2] more effectively.

3 In the fight against terrorism, western governments want to stop extremists from corrupting / corruption the minds of the young.

4 The national media is largely responsible / responsibility [1] for giving people a false perception / perceptive [2] of what the European Commission does. In fact, Brussels plays a purely advise / advisory [3] role.

5 Democratic governments can advice / advise [1] and even recommend / recommendation [2], but they have no right to interfere / interfering [3] in the private lives of their citizens.

6 This article about state interfere / interference [1] in our personal affairs is very perceive / perceptive [2]. I learnt a lot from it.

5 BUILDING SKILLS: QUALIFYING OPINIONS

›› SB page 112, exercise 3

Eric and Martin are talking about the EU. Complete their discussion with the phrases from the box

as far as I can see | I get the impression that | It is absolutely clear | On the contrary, the fact is | On the whole, I suppose that | the opposite is true | There can be absolutely no doubt | This fact seems to suggest that

Eric: I'm so fed up with European bureaucrats telling us what to do all the time. I think the EU is just a waste of taxpayers' money.

Martin: Well, ______________________ [1], there are quite a few benefits from the EU. The EU can fight international crime better than national governments can, for example.

Eric: I don't believe that for a moment. ______________________ [2] to me that we would be better off without the EU. Just look at all that money they spend on translating everything into all the languages.

Martin: Well, that is a problem, of course. But from listening to the news, ______________________ [3] the politicians want to limit the number of languages used.

Eric: No, ______________________ [4]: every country insists on having everything in its own language.

Martin: ______________________ [5] it does cost a lot of money, but it is necessary, I think. But I'm conviced the EU does help: where would we be if people couldn't move from one country to another to get a job.

Eric: I don't really agree with you at all. ______________________ [6] that all these people moving around the continent are just pushing down wages. ______________________ [7] that we would have more money to spend if there weren't so many immigrants taking our jobs away.

Martin: I can't agree with you there. ______________________ [8] the free movement of labour creates more jobs and is better for the economy.

6 WORDFIELD: WORD COMPLETION

A Put the missing vowels into the words and expressions you need to talk about the EU.

1 C_RR_PT__N
2 _NT_RF_R_NC_
3 _ND_M_CR_T_C
4 B_R___CR_TS
5 P_RC_PT__N
6 __R_P__N C_MM_SS__N
7 N_T__N_L G_V_RNM_NTS
8 L_G_SL_T_VE P_W_R
9 C__NC_L _F M_N_ST_RS
10 M_MB_R ST_T_

B Complete the sentences with five of the words / expressions you have found.

1 A lot of people do not understand that the ______________________[1] has no ______________________[2] at all. It can only advise and recommend.

2 A big problem is that the ______________________[1] is made up of the heads of the ______________________[2].

3 The media is full of stories of corrupt ______________________[1] in Brussels but in fact ______________________[2] are responsible for paying out money to farmers, for example. It is all a question of ______________________[3], not reality.

7 TECHNICAL OPTIONS

›› SB page 113

This is a speed test. Write down as quickly as you can which shape in Group 2 is identical to the shape in Group 1.

Group 1

Group 2

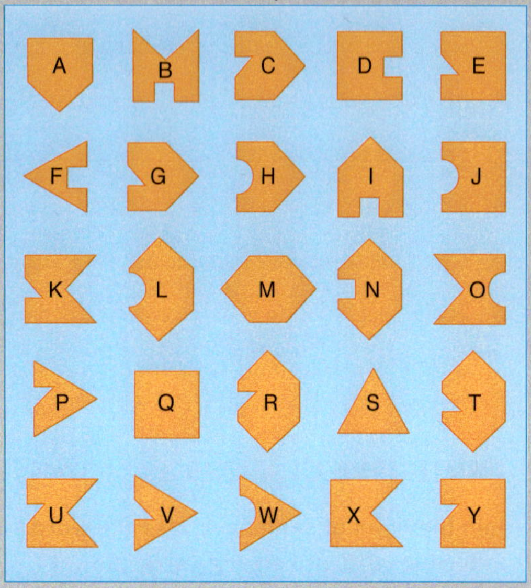

1 *X*	6 ______	11 ______	16 ______	21 ______
2 *P*	7 ______	12 ______	17 ______	22 ______
3 ______	8 ______	13 ______	18 ______	23 ______
4 ______	9 ______	14 ______	19 ______	24 ______
5 ______	10 ______	15 ______	20 ______	25 ______

9 Social challenges

1 VOCABULARY

›› SB page 116, text; page 119, text

**A Create opposites of these words from the Section A and B texts.
Use your dictionary if necessary to help you choose from the following prefixes.**

de- | dis- | il- | im- | in- | ir- | mis- | un-

Section A text

1 perfect ______
2 tidy ______
3 responsible ______
4 prove ______
5 possible ______
6 believe ______

Section B text

7 action ______
8 understand ______
9 direct ______
10 attention ______
11 use ______
12 decrease ______

B Use pairs of words from A and B to complete the following. Change their forms if necessary.

1 We need a free press to check that politicians ______[1] their power well and do not ______[2] it by acting dishonestly.

2 Parents who do not care for their children are very ______[1] , and are often partly ______[2] for their children's future problems.

3 The WHO plans strong ______[1] against malaria as ______[2] would mean the deaths of millions more, including many children.

4 As many young people grow up, family influence ______[1] , and peer group pressure to join gangs ______[2] .

5 People often see their role models as ______[1] in every way, but role models are only human, and all humans are very ______[2] .

6 Some people fail to vote because they think it is ______[1] to change society. But others feel that voting is their only ______[2] way of getting a better government.

2 PARTICIPLE CLAUSES 1

›› SB page 124, Grammar checkpoint

Join the pairs of sentences. Use the word in brackets with the correct sentence and change the following verb into an *-ing* participle.

1 You are legally allowed to gamble at casinos in the USA. You reach the age of 18. *(after)*.

You are legally allowed to gamble at casinos in the USA after reaching the age of 18.

2 Tracy Parr grew up in Sandpoint, Idaho. She learned that various family members enjoyed a little gambling. *(when)*

______

______

3 She reached her 18th birthday. She immediately drove with her boyfriend, Carl, to the nearest casino. *(on)*

4 She lost $5 - a small price for a lot of fun, she thought. She played every machine in the place that evening. *(while)*

5 She left the casino to go home that night. She had already become a gambling addict. *(before)*

6 She spent more and more time at the casino in the following months. She sometimes won but usually lost - and could never stop. *(while)*

7 She nearly went to prison. She stole money from work to feed her addiction. *(after)*

8 She thought there was no escape from gambling. She finally joined a group called Gamblers Anonymous which showed her the way out. *(before)*

3 PARTICIPLE CLAUSES 2

›› SB page 124, Grammar checkpoint

Change the relative clauses (starting with *who*, *which*, *that*) to *-ing* or *-ed* participle clauses. Rewrite the text in your exercise book.

Dr Louisa Piper is a psychologist **who is trained** as a therapist and **who now specializes** in the area of family problems. She helps family members who have difficulties in their relationships. She says the problems that face them are often caused by outside stresses. For example, she often sees parents who are forced to work very long hours to earn enough money. That can badly affect children who grow up in this lonely environment. The personal problems that are created by such pressures come in many forms. She gives as an example one family that has been badly damaged in this way. There is an 18-year-old daughter who was recently taken to hospital with severe anorexia. There is also a 15-year-old daughter who is staying out late at night and who is spending time with known troublemakers. And there is a 10-year-old son who is too frightened to leave the house at all. Piper is now setting the family challenges that are designed to bring them together. For instance, Sunday evening has become a 'fun family time' which requires them all to spend time together on a shared family activity.

Start like this:
*Dr Louisa Piper is a psychologist **trained** as a therapist and now **specializing** in the area of family problems.*

4 ARTICLES

›› SB page 124, Grammar checkpoint

Add *a/an* or *the* where necessary. Write *x* where no article is needed.

Steffie Kaufman, animal rights activist

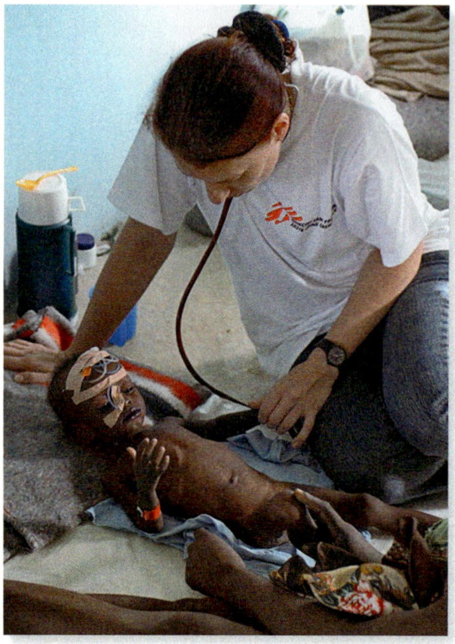

As _a_ [1] child at _x_ [2] school, Steffie was always very good at ____ [3] science. When she was still very young, she decided that she would like to go to ____ [4] college and become ____ [5] doctor. However, she also loved ____ [6] animals, she read all ____ [7] books about ____ [8] zoology that she could find, and she often wondered whether to become ____ [9] vet* instead. She changed her mind ____ [10] thousand times, but finally she applied to go to ____ [11] medical school. However, as ____ [12] student she soon became ____ [13] animal rights activist, and one night she went with ____ [14] group of ____ [15] students to free all ____ [16] animals kept for ____ [17] animal experiments at the university's science laboratories. She and some of ____ [18] other activists were caught by ____ [19] police, and they were told to appear in ____ [20] court ____ [21] few weeks later. There, they were each ordered to do ____ [22] hundred hours of ____ [23] community service. Since getting her medical qualifications, Steffie has been working for ____ [24] World Health Organization in ____ [25] central Africa in the long fight to control ____ [26] tropical diseases like ____ [27] malaria. There are ____ [28] lot of endangered animal species in that part of ____ [29] world and, not surprisingly, Steffie is also doing ____ [30] work in her free time to help protect species in danger such as ____ [31] famous silver-back gorilla.

***vet:** short for 'veterinarian' (= *Tierarzt/-ärztin*)

5 WORDFIELD: SOCIAL CHALLENGES

A Find 20 words in the word square.

A	G	O	V	E	R	N	M	E	N	T	W	X	W	M	B	P	M	A	B	A	N	D	O	N
P	E	S	X	T	A	I	K	L	T	P	R	E	S	S	U	R	E	D	Y	N	Q	P	W	P
E	L	E	C	T	I	O	N	M	B	W	E	R	L	I	E	T	R	M	W	V	N	O	R	E
T	V	R	W	C	H	S	I	S	O	C	I	A	L	I	Z	E	G	O	E	I	P	L	S	M
R	M	E	A	N	S	T	S	G	E	R	S	P	L	C	B	N	R	V	N	O	M	I	T	O
E	D	L	U	S	D	R	A	D	D	I	C	T	I	O	N	T	X	E	C	L	Y	C	M	T
L	Y	A	P	O	L	U	V	M	W	E	K	L	E	Q	T	E	C	M	B	E	P	I	E	I
I	K	T	L	C	N	C	P	O	L	I	T	I	C	I	A	N	M	E	W	N	T	E	I	O
G	M	I	A	I	P	T	W	R	C	A	Y	Q	W	E	P	C	M	N	T	C	R	S	Z	N
I	Y	V	M	E	Y	U	N	C	A	M	P	A	I	G	N	E	L	T	S	E	W	I	E	A
O	I	E	X	T	E	R	B	R	I	D	E	Z	T	G	U	I	C	I	D	R	U	G	A	L
N	A	I	L	Y	W	E	H	G	M	E	D	I	A	O	P	L	H	E	W	O	X	K	C	L
A	C	H	I	L	D	C	A	R	E	X	N	D	E	M	O	N	S	T	R	A	T	I	O	N

B Now complete the following sentences with words from the word square.

1 Women fought a long ____________________ for the right to vote.

2 Women's traditional roles were ____________________ and making a home.

3 If a child's parents cannot look after it, this role is sometimes accepted by ____________________ such as grandparents.

4 One of today's greatest causes of social problems is drug ____________________ .

5 The job of a ____________________ is to be a strong voice for the people who voted for him or her.

6 Yesterday, there was a big ____________________ against the government. About 100,000 people came to march through the capital.

6 TECHNICAL OPTIONS

›› SB page 123

Read the speech bubbles and choose a person from the box to say who is talking.

cook | customer adviser | satisfied younger customer | sceptical older customer | washer-up | worried waiter

1 *Well, the food was OK, but I much prefer the human touch. Everything's run by computers nowadays, and now this!*

____

4 *First we got self-service restaurants and now automated ones. But what about people like me? I'll be out of a job.*

____

2 *My job's safe, I suppose. Thank heavens they haven't found a way to prepare food automatically yet.*

____

5 *I find it really cool. It's a lot of fun and the food's good, too. I'll definitely come again.*

____

3 *The food is ordered and served automatically, but we still have to collect and wash the dirty plates and so on.*

____

6 *Let me help you. Choose your meal and then just touch the icon on the screen with your finger. The computer does everything else.*

____

10 Multiculturalism

1 BUILDING SKILLS: DESCRIBING ILLUSTRATIONS

›› SB page 125, Focus

Use the text plan to describe the drawing of a street market on page 125 of the Student's Book in detail. Write in an exercise book. Add any other details you may see.

In the	foreground	there	is	a	boy(s)	wearing a	hijab.
	middle distance	you can	are	an	girl(s)	with	turban.
	background		see	some	children		sari.
				two	older people		jacket.
				three	younger people		jeans.
				...	old man/men		long hair.
					young woman/women		shaved head.
					black/white		
					Muslim/Sikh		

On the right	there is a	fruit stall.
On the left		grocery stall / shop.
In the middle		church / town hall.
		clock tower.
		street lamp.

A	stallholder	is	looking at	a	bag.
An	older man	are	selling	an	fruit.
The	boys		laughing	some	friends.
			carrying		shopping trolley.
			talking		customers.
			holding		
			pushing		

In the foreground in the middle there are two boys. They are laughing. There is a fruit stall on the left. Two older people are buying some fruit from the stall-holder. In the background ...

2 CONNECTORS

›› SB pages 126–127, text

Underline the correct connector.

Hanif Kureishi, who / whose [1] father is Pakistani and mother English, was born in the London suburb of Bromley. After / When [2] leaving Bromley Technical High School, he spent a year at Lancaster University before / but [3] dropping out. However / Moreover [4], he later went to London University and / but [5] got a degree in philosophy.

His first novel, called *The Buddha of Suburbia*, won a prize and / furthermore [6] was also made into a successful TV series. His next major novel, *Intimacy*, about a man leaving his wife and two young sons because / because of [7] his wife's coldness caused surprise as / while [8] Kureishi himself had recently left his wife and two young sons.

In fact / Therefore [9], the autobiographical nature of Kureishi's work caused big problems. This was because / due to [10] his family felt that he made unfair use of them in his novels by / from [11] "selling them for his own profit".

Hanif's sister, Yasmin, was particularly bitter on account of / because [12] the autobiographical content of *The Buddha of Suburbia*, in which / which [13] the Buddha is an obvious portrait of her father. Although / As a consequence [14] Yasmin wrote to a newspaper saying that her father was so angry that / therefore [15] he didn't speak to Hanif for nearly a year.

3 REPORTED SPEECH: STATEMENTS

›› SB page 134, Grammar checkpoint

Rewrite the statements for a newspaper report on illegal immigration into Spain. Use the introductory verbs in brackets.

1 

Minister: "The Spanish government is doing all it can to stop illegal immigration, but we cannot do the job alone. The rest of the EU must help us." *(tell reporters; add)*

Speaking in English, the Spanish interior minister ______________________________

2 

Dr Sanchez: "We have found that Spain needs some skilled immigrants, but unfortunately the illegals are almost all unskilled. Most can't even understand Spanish." *(say; point out)*

Dr Sanchez, an economist, ______________________________

3 

Julia Gonzales: "The anti-immigrant feeling in Spain has been made much worse by the media, which always exaggerates the number of people who are coming here." *(think)*

Julia Gonzales ______________________________

4 

Priest: "People think that African immigrants just want to come to Spain to have a better life, but I see it as a humanitarian problem. The fact is that these people have no life at all where they come from." *(emphasize; conclude by saying)*

A priest ______________________________

4 REPORTED SPEECH: QUESTIONS

›› SB page 134, Grammar checkpoint

Some high school students are asking a visitor from the UN refugee agency about the organization and its work. Report the students' questions for the school magazine. Use the introductory verbs in brackets.

1 "When was the UN refugee agency founded?" *(ask)*

Eli ______________________ the UN refugee agency ______________________ .

2 "What is the main role of the agency?" *(want to know)*

Joshua ______________________ of the agency ______________________ .

3 "Does the head of the agency have to come from a neutral country like Switzerland?" *(wonder)*

Helen ______________________ the head of the agency ______________________

a neutral country like Switzerland.

4 "Is the agency's head office in New York?" *(ask)*

Grant ______________________ in New York.

5 "In how many countries does the agency have an office?" *(want to know)*

Julie ______________________

6 "What is the biggest problem facing the refugee agency?" *(enquire)*

David ______________________

5 REPORTED SPEECH: REQUESTS

›› SB page 134, Grammar checkpoint

A border guard stops a truck that has just crossed the US-Mexican border into California. He thinks the Mexican driver may be carrying illegal immigrants. Report what the guards tells the driver to do. Use the introductory verbs in brackets.

1 "Switch off the engine." *(tell + the driver)*

The guard ______________________ .

2 "Get out of the cab." *(ask + him)*

He ______________________ .

3 "Give me your driver's license and other documents." *(request + the man)*

The guard ______________________

______________________ .

4 "Open the doors at the back of the truck and don't touch anything." *(order + the Mexican)*

He ______________________

______________________ .

5 "Unload some cases and show me what's behind them." *(instruct + the driver)*

He ______________________

______________________ .

6 "Don't put your hands in your pockets. Keep them where I can see them" (tell + the man)

The guard ______________________

but ______________________ .

6 WORDFIELD: MULTICULTURALISM

›› SB page 129, text

Use the clues to solve the puzzle and find the key word.

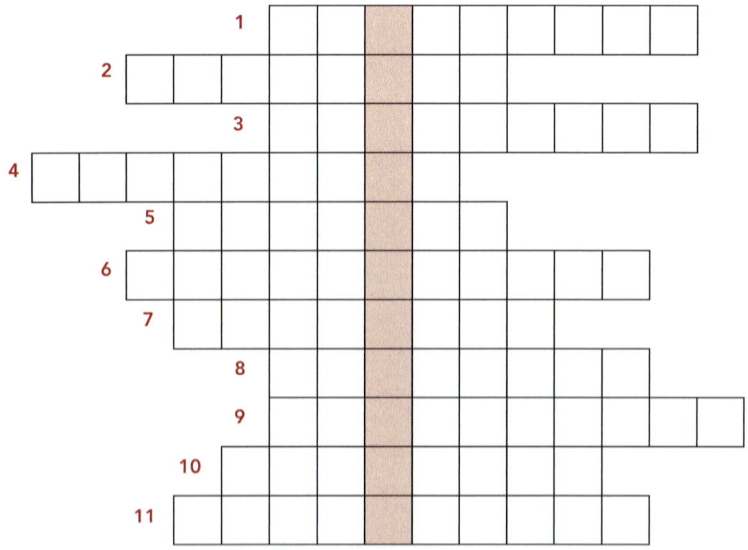

The key word is

______________________________ .

1 person who goes to another country to live there permanently
2 the way that people think about something is their ... to it
3 Leo Jimenez's original nationality
4 noun form of adjective "ethnic"
5 accepted style of clothing, hair, make up etc, particularly among women
6 person who studies changes in population trends
7 adjective meaning person of Spanish heritage
8 a person's family background going back a long way in time
9 noun meaning "always the same"
10 enormously successful entertainment star like, for example, Jennifer Lopez
11 noun form of adjective "popular"

7 TECHNICAL OPTIONS

›› SB page 133

Use the labelled drawing on Student's Book page 133 to describe a DART buoy and how it works.

acoustic transducer | anchors | antenna | coastal communities | data | earth's surface | electronic systems | radio signals | 'sea-side' | seismographic stations | surface buoy | tsunami information

Other than the ______________________________[1] itself, the main components of a DART buoy are the ______________________________[2], batteries and an ______________________________[3] mounted on its upper or "air-side" surface. The lower or ______________________________[4] surface of the buoy is fitted with an ______________________________[5] that can receive and transmit ______________________________[6]. The equipment is held in place by ______________________________[7] on the seabed.

The acoustic transducer continuously receives ______________________________[8] about movements of the ______________________________[9] beneath the sea from a further transducer on the seabed. This data is then transmitted via satellite to ______________________________[10] on land. From there, it is sent on to national ______________________________[11] centres that can send out warnings to ______________________________[12] at risk.

Crime

1 VOCABULARY

›› SB page 135, Focus

A Fit a crime from the box to the definitions 1–10.

armed robbery | burglary | drunk driving | graffiti-spraying | manslaughter | mugging | murder | rape | shoplifting | terrorism

1 blowing up, for example, a train to make a political or religious statement ______

2 entering, for example a bank with a gun and demanding money ______

3 causing another person's death without intending to do so ______

4 having sexual intercourse without the other person's consent ______

5 painting designs on buildings without the owner's consent ______

6 removing goods from a store without paying for them ______

7 intentionally taking sb's life after careful planning ______

8 breaking into a building to steal sb's property ______

9 attacking sb in the street to steal their bag, wallet ______

10 being in charge of a vehicle while under the influence of alcohol ______

B How serious are the above crimes? Sort the crimes into a column that gives your own opinion and then use the material to say why.

Very serious	Serious	Not so serious

2 GRAMMAR: ADVERB ORDER

›› SB page 144, Grammar checkpoint

Use arrows to put the adverbs of frequency into the sentences.

1 I'm afraid the police don't patrol the streets. very frequently

2 Liberal commentators claim that poverty causes crime. always

3 Harsh punishment stops people from committing crimes. seldom

4 I enjoy a good crime novel. now and then

5 There is an increase in street crime at Christmas. usually

6 Unfortunately, people leave valuables in their cars. sometimes

7 There's no point in reporting trivial crimes to the police. often

8 You should lock the doors. every night

3 GRAMMAR: WORD ORDER

›› SB page 144, Grammar checkpoint

Spot the mistake: All the sentences have one word order mistake. Use arrows to correct it.

1 The prime minister is opening the new Marsh Prison tomorrow in Leeds.

2 Prime ministers usually do not open prisons, but this is a particularly important occasion.

3 Marsh Prison is different from traditional prisons completely.

4 Marsh Prison is more like a hotel than a fortress unlike traditional prisons.

5 The cells are bigger for example and have a separate toilet and shower like in a hotel.

6 Each cell is just occupied by one prisoner.

7 And prisoners only will spend twelve hours a day in their cells.

8 Prisoners will spend the rest of their time usually doing a useful job or job training.

9 Some conservatives complain of course that prisoners are not on holiday.

10 But supporters say that we must find an answer in traditional prisons to the problem of suicide.

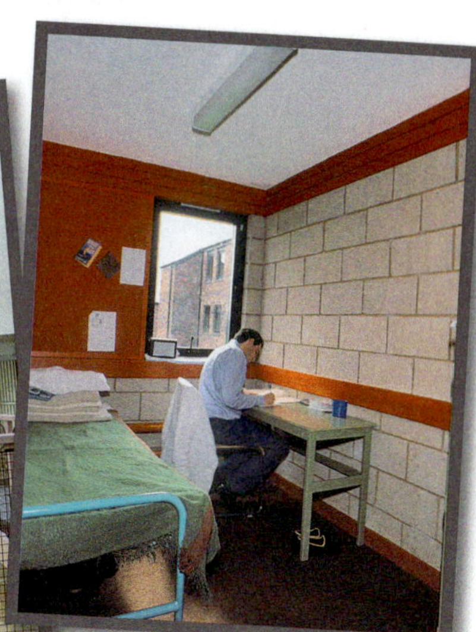

4 BUILDING SKILLS: GIVING A TALK

›› SB page 141, exercise 4

You are giving a talk on the death penalty in the USA. You introduce your talk by referring to the bar chart below about American public opinion on this issue. Read the jumbled sentences 1–8 and use the numbers to link them to the bar chart.

1 At 60 % in favour, the figure for Independents was between these two extremes.

2 Finally, let's look at religion. Here, at 71 % for capital punishment, white protestants were well above the national average, while at 67 % white catholics were not quite so sure.

3 People without any formal religious affiliation voted 59 % in favour.

4 For all that, the biggest differences were found in opinion for or against by political affiliation.

5 However, the survey found big differences by racial, political and religious affiliation (*Zugehörigkeit*).

6 For example, while 78 % of Republicans were in favour of capital punishment, this applied to only 49 % of Democrats.

7 In the survey, 62 % of all respondents were in favour of the death penalty, and 32 % opposed it.

8 Looking at race first, while 68% of whites favoured the death penalty, only 40 % of blacks did so.

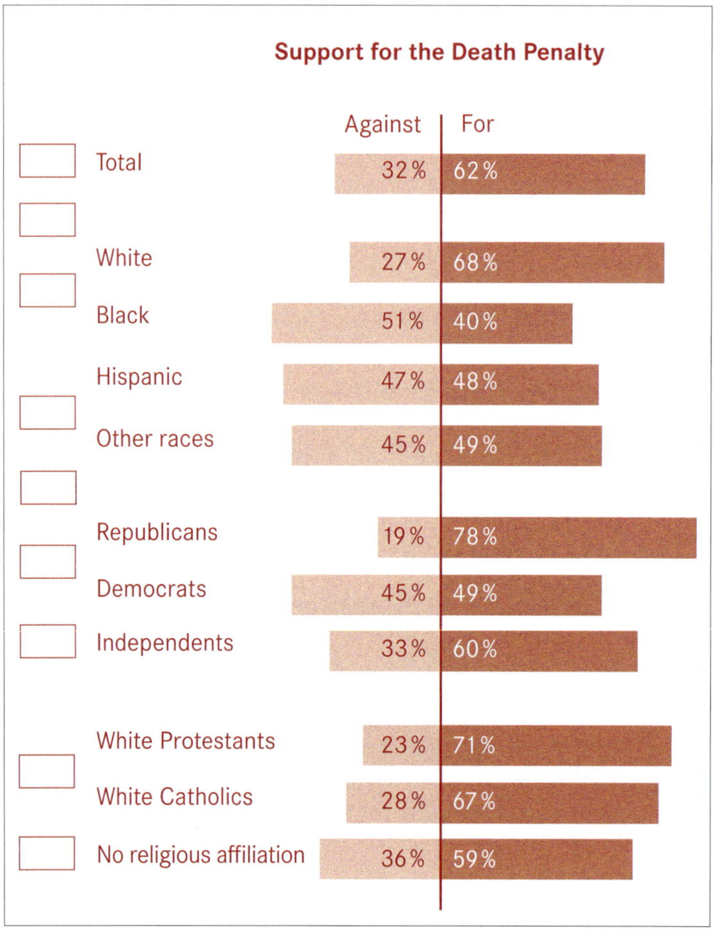

Source: *Pew Research Center 2007*

9 The result for Hispanics was 48 % for and 47 % against, and that for people of other races was 49 % and 45 % respectively.

5 WORDFIELD: CRIME

Find the English equivalents of these German words in the wordsquare on page 59.

1 Abschreckung ______________________

2 bestechlich ______________________

3 Bestechung ______________________

4 gnadenlos ______________________

5 Ladendieb ______________________

6 Mord ______________________

7 New Yorker Polizeibehörde (Abkürzung) ______________________

8 Rassismus ______________________

9 Raubüberfall ______________________

10 Strafmaß ______________________

11 Toleranz ______________________

12 Vergewaltigung ______________________

M	E	R	C	I	L	E	S	S	B	O	L	G	A	V
I	U	T	M	W	E	N	O	O	B	X	F	A	E	S
E	N	R	P	R	O	L	S	E	N	T	E	N	C	E
A	B	V	D	S	H	U	H	A	D	E	S	V	I	S
H	T	H	I	E	N	T	O	L	E	R	A	N	C	E
I	U	F	S	K	R	E	P	E	A	G	S	I	O	T
B	R	I	B	E	R	Y	L	C	E	D	D	Y	R	S
V	O	C	H	E	S	A	I	P	L	U	M	B	R	E
O	B	E	A	T	H	S	F	E	M	O	I	S	U	T
B	B	P	I	L	M	S	T	P	A	R	N	Y	P	D
M	E	F	I	E	G	E	E	A	C	L	O	T	T	R
N	R	I	D	E	T	E	R	R	E	N	T	D	A	T
P	Y	S	C	H	P	R	I	O	F	S	I	D	A	X

You have to look in these directions!

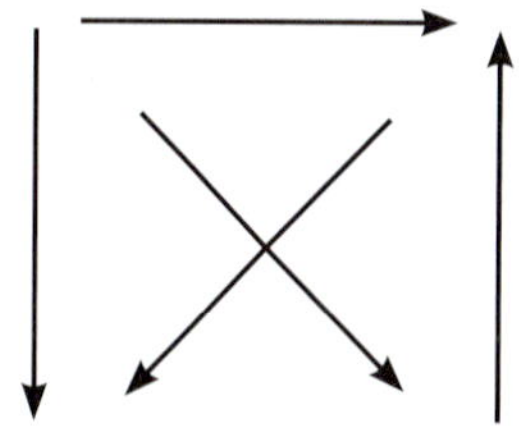

6 TECHNICAL OPTIONS

›› SB page 143

Study the labelled drawing of a basic mobile phone. Then complete the descriptive text.

Key

1 Power switch
2 Earpiece (speaker)
3 Volume +/- buttons
4 Left/Right selection buttons
5 Select menu button
6 Clear display button
7 Call button
8 End call button
9 Scroll button
10 Keypad

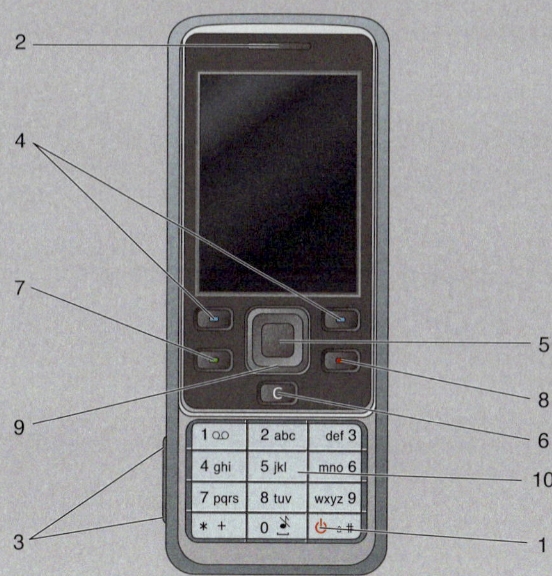

The ______________________[1] is at the very top of the front panel.

The control buttons are grouped together immediately below the display (*Bildschirm*). These controls consist of two ______________________[2] buttons, the select ______________________[3] button and the ______________________[4] button. The remaining control buttons are the ______________________[5] button on the left and the ______________________[6] button on the right. In between is the button to ______________________[7] menus.

The ______________________[8] is used for keying in numbers or writing text messages. The ______________________[9] is located at the bottom right of these keys.

Finally, the ______________________[10] buttons are situated on the side of the phone at the bottom left.

Future life, future living

1 VOCABULARY: DEFINITIONS

›› SB page 146, text

A Link a word/expression from the box with a definition.

announce | astonishing | ban | boycott | calf | current | derive from sth. | ingredient | offspring | onset | prematurely | vast quantity

1 refusal to trade in a product, usually for ethical reasons ____________
2 the young of an animal ____________
3 adjective meaning 'present' in the sense of 'now' ____________
4 make public in speech or writing ____________
5 have its origins in sth. ____________
6 noun meaning 'veto' ____________
7 (here) product that goes into food ____________
8 adjective meaning 'extremely surprising' ____________
9 (here) young of a cow ____________
10 synonym for 'huge amount' ____________
11 adverb meaning 'earlier than expected or planned' ____________
12 noun meaning 'beginning', 'start' ____________

B Complete the sentences with a word from the box.

1 Many countries have introduced a ____________ on smoking in public places.
2 Personal names like 'Baker' and 'Miller' ____________ the names of jobs.
3 We can learn a lot from elephants. They raise their ____________ together.
4 Do you have a ____________ bus timetable, please?
5 Susan's baby was born ____________ but it is going to be fine.
6 It's ____________ that the central banks didn't notice what was happening.

2 VOCABULARY: COLLOCATIONS

›› SB page 146, text

Form collocations by adding a noun from the box to the nouns in the list.
⚠ Collocation: Two nouns, e.g. 'fruit juice', 'fillet steak', that are often used together.

~~animals~~ | calf | farming | fiction | herd | infection | laws | officials | suffering | talks

1 farm *animals*
2 emergency ____________
3 EU ____________
4 health ____________
5 Holstein ____________
6 clone ____________
7 science ____________
8 dairy ____________
9 animal ____________
10 lung ____________

3 MULTIPLE MATCHING: SPEAKERS AND STATEMENTS

›› SB page 149–150, text

Match the speakers A–H to the statements 1–8.

A	Alison Fox, eco-activist	E	Helen Bond, company executive
B	Brian Moore, vegetable grower	F	Ken Oldham, supermarket buyer
C	Dr Harry Sutton, biologist	G	Sarah Clarke, government health official
D	Dr Susan Edwards, family doctor	H	Ted Davis, dairy farmer

1. To ensure the health of our herd, we only allow our best cows to breed. ☐
2. From my point of view as a grower, the biggest commercial advantage of GM tomatoes is that they do not need so much expensive fertilizer. ☐
3. GM farming could be a disaster because nobody can say how GM plants interact with natural ones. ☐
4. My colleagues and I are very worried that the antibiotic-resistant genes in GM plants could reduce the effectiveness of the antibiotics we use in medicine. ☐
5. In spite of all the dramatic warnings in the media, in fact there's no evidence that GM food has bad effects. ☐
6. We sell GM fruit and vegetables mainly because it has a longer shelf life. That makes business sense. ☐
7. I don't know what consumers are so worried about, frankly. GM food is subject to very strict regulation to ensure that it is safe. ☐
8. Universal Biotech Inc. is spending millions of dollars on solving the problem of 'superweeds', and I'm sure we'll succeed. ☐

4 BUILDING SKILLS: TRANSLATING ENGLISH INTO GERMAN

Translate the sentences into German. Take special care with the highlighted parts.

1 Unfortunately, we have made little progress towards controlling cloning.

____

2 Several pieces of valuable furniture were damaged in the fire.

____

3 The news about the cloning of humans is terrifying.

____

4 You will find a lot of information on cloning on the internet, but some of it is nonsense.

____

5 Not all the scientists that are doing cloning experiments are responsible.

____

6 The doctor has told me to eat less and do more exercise in future.

____

7 Bob has been studying biology ever since he was able to read.

____

8 The university stopped the experiments because several scientists were breaking the law.

____

9 It is said that human life will be completely changed by advances in medicine.

____

10 It is feared that even more digitalization could lead to a complete loss of privacy.

____

5 GRAMMAR PROBLEMS

›› SB page 154, Grammar checkpoint

Cross out the incorrect alternative.

1 My ex and I live in the same village. I can't avoid meeting/to meet him sometimes, can I?
2 You'll find two pairs of scissors/scissors in the drawer.
3 Is that the man which/who caused the accident?
4 We're looking forward to come/coming to your party on Saturday.
5 Jack didn't go/hasn't gone on holiday last year because he was ill.
6 I am/have been at this school for two years now.
7 My mum and dad are flying/fly to Florida this afternoon.
8 I am waiting/have been waiting to see the doctor for nearly three hours now.
9 Anna Netrebko sings the role of Violetta wonderfully/wonderfully the role of Violetta.
10 The Bartons live in Station Road in the flats/in the flats in Station Road.
11 We had an ice cream while we waited/were waiting for the movie to start.
12 I am cycling/cycle to school every day.
13 Jane is going to work/will work as a sales assistant in the summer.
14 If you won a lot of money, what will you do/would you do?
15 I'd like six slices ham/slices of ham, please.
16 The traffic jam was caused by sheep/sheeps on the road.
17 The driver would have lived if the ambulance would come/had come more quickly.
18 My brother had to do/must do two years in the army when he was 18.
19 Would you like to try on these shoes or those ones/shoes?
20 My computer was made/was make in China.

6 WORDFIELD: WORD SNAKES

Divide up the letters into words and insert the missing punctuation to make correct sentences.

atendencytogetillnessessuchascanceranddiabetesisprogrammedbyapersonsDNA

foodpoisoningisoftencausedbysomebodyscarelessnessbetweenthefarmgateandthesupermarketshelf

7 TECHNICAL OPTIONS

›› SB page 153

Look at Student's Book page 153 again, then finish translating these sentences about robotic surgery into English.

1 *Man hofft, dass die Anwendung von Robotern die Kosten der medizinischen Versorgung reduzieren wird.*

It is hoped ______ medical care.

2 *Die Roboterchirurgie bedeutet weniger Schmerz und viel kürzere Genesungszeiten für Patienten.*

Robotic surgery ______ .

3 *Fortschritte in der Roboterchirurgie werden radikale Veränderungen bei Herzoperationen verursachen.*

Advances ______ .

4 *Bei konventionellen Herzbypassoperationen muss der Brustkorb des Patienten mit einer 30 cm-langen Inzision geöffnet werden.*

In conventional heart bypass operations ______ .

5 *Mit Hilfe eines Roboterarms ist es möglich, diese Operation mit drei genau plazierten Inzisionen von nur 1 cm durchzuführen.*

With the help of a robotic arm ______ .

6 *Keine menschliche Hand kann der Beständigkeit eines Roboterarms gleichkommen.*

No human hand ______ .

Internal combustion engines

1 A 4-STROKE INTERNAL COMBUSTION ENGINE

›› SB pages 156–157

Label the cylinder of a 4-stroke internal combustion engine with words/expressions from the box.

camshaft | combustion chamber | crank case | crank chamber | crankshaft | cylinder block | cylinder head | exhaust valve | fuel intake | intake valve | piston | spark plug

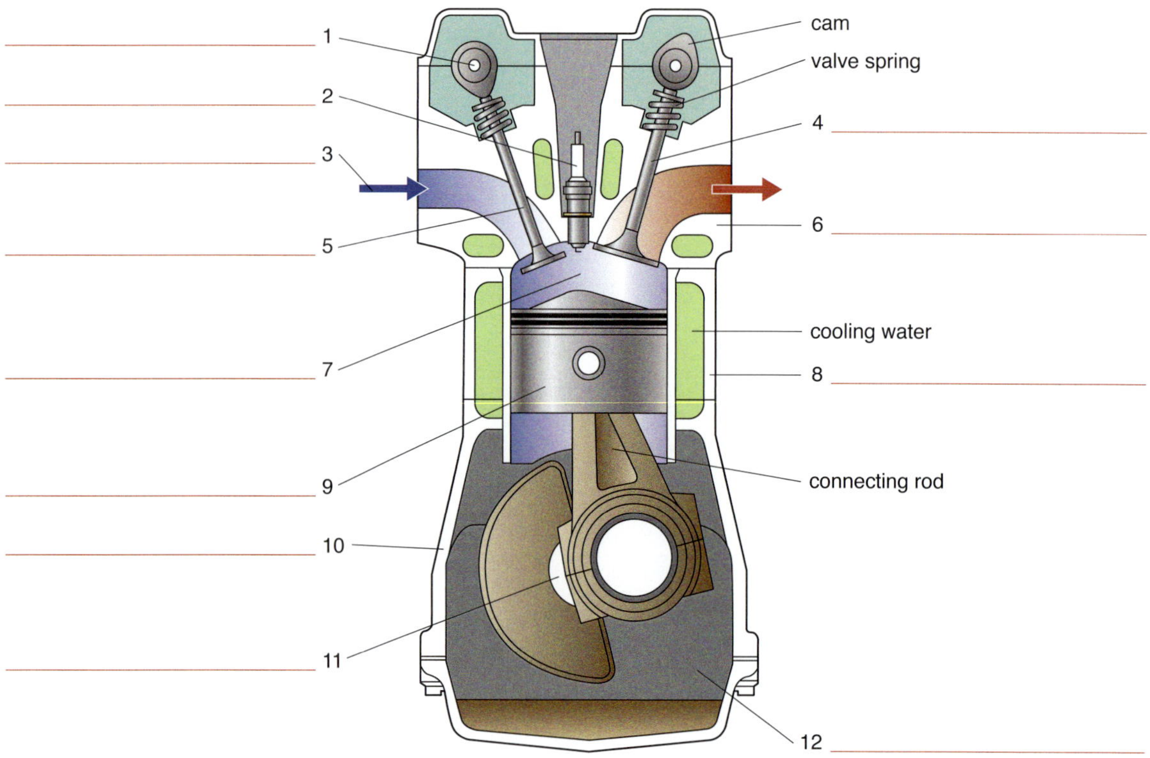

2 PARTS OF AN ENGINE

›› SB pages 156–157

Link the engine parts on the left to their function on the right.

1 camshaft	☐	a	causes fuel/air mixture to explode in combustion chamber
2 connecting rod *(Kurbelstange)*	☐	b	closes the exhaust valve when cam releases it
3 cooling water	☐	c	opens/closes valves at correct time in cycle
4 cylinder head	☐	d	stops engine from overheating
5 spark plug	☐	e	assembly (*Konstruktion*) on top of cylinder block fitted with spark plugs and valves
6 crankshaft	☐	f	stop loss of pressure between pistons and cylinder walls
7 piston rings *(Kolbenringe)*	☐	g	transfers vertical movement of piston to crankschaft
8 valve spring *(Feder)*	☐	h	converts vertical movement into rotation

3 AN ENGINE QUIZ

›› SB pages 156–157

Do the *engine quiz* by choosing the correct alternative a), b) or c).

1 An internal combustion engine is useful because it converts ...

a ☐ fuel into heat. b ☐ fuel into motion. c ☐ fuel into exhaust gases.

2 In 4-stroke engines, the strokes are ...

a ☐ intake – compression – ignition – exhaust.
b ☐ injection – rotation – ignition – exhaust.
c ☐ injection – carburetion – rotation – exhaust.

3 The function of the crankshaft is to ...

a ☐ deliver fuel to the cylinders.
b ☐ change vertical motion into rotational motion.
c ☐ keep cylinder heads in place.

4 A normal internal combustion engine runs smoothly because ...

a ☐ the fuel/air mixture is ignited by the spark plug.
b ☐ the crankshaft stores energy and releases it slowly.
c ☐ the explosion in each cylinder takes place at a different time.

5 The three faults that can cause an engine not to start are a bad fuel mix, a lack of compression and a lack of ...

a ☐ exhaust. b ☐ water. c ☐ spark.

6 The intake and exhaust valves are operated by the ...

a ☐ camshaft. b ☐ connecting rod. c ☐ piston.

7 When the ignition key is turned, the starter motor ...

a ☐ sends electricity to the spark plugs, starting ignition.
b ☐ pre-compresses the fuel/air mixture.
c ☐ turns the engine a few revolutions, starting the combustion process.

4 TESTING USEFUL ENGINE POWER

›› SB page 158

Complete the sentences with words or expressions from page 158 of the Student's Book.

1 The term 'useful engine power' relates ______________ to engine speed.

2 A ______________ measures engine performance.

3 A simple dynanometer consists of a ______________ [1] suspended from a ______________ [2] over a wheel.

4 The mass and strap act as a ______________ [1] on the ______________ [2] by generating friction.

5 The braking effect produced by ______________ [1] acts against engine ______________ [2].

6 Useful engine power can be calculated by using a ______________.

7 In the past, the useful engine power was given in ______________ or 'bhp'.

8 Nowadays, engine power is given in ______________ [1], 1 bhp being standardized at ______________ [2] Watts.

Electricity

1 ELECTRICITY DISTRIBUTION

›› SB page 160, exercise 1

A Complete the table with the English equivalents of the German terms.

	German	English
1	*Wohnungen*	
2	*elektrische Spannung*	
3	*Elektrizität erzeugen*	
4	*Fabrik*	
5	*Freileitung*	
6	*Kraftwerk*	
7	*leiten*	
8	*Leitungsmast*	
9	*umspannen*	
10	*Umspannwerk*	

B Now complete the sentences with words from the table. Be careful about plural forms.

We ____________[1] most of our electricity in ____________[2] and distribute it through ____________[3], which are usually supported on ____________[4]. Electricity companies ____________[5] electricity to a lower ____________[6] at ____________[7] before they ____________[8] it to domestic ____________[9] and ____________[10].

2 ELECTRICAL CIRCUITS

›› SB page 161, exercise 3

Study the electrical circuit right and then answer the questions on page 67 by choosing the correct alternative.

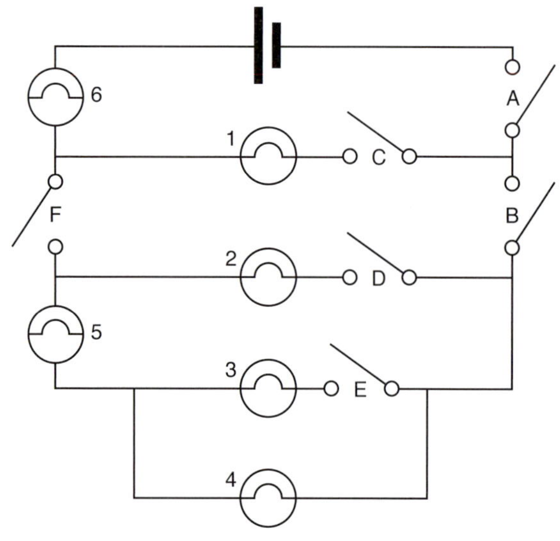

1 Which bulbs will light up if only switches A, B, D and F are closed?
Tip: Close the four switches with a pencil line and then trace the path of the current in colour.

a ☐ bulbs 1, 2, 5 and 6　　b ☐ only bulbs 2 and 6
c ☐ bulbs 2, 4, 5 and 6　　d ☐ bulbs 2, 3, 4, 5 and 6

2 Which bulbs will light up if only switches B, C, D and F are closed?

a ☐ bulbs 2, 4, 5 and 6　　b ☐ bulbs 2, 3 and 5
c ☐ bulbs 1, 2, 4, 5 and 6　　d ☐ none of them

3 Which single switch is the 'master switch' that can turn all of the bulbs off?

a ☐ A　　b ☐ F　　c ☐ B

4 If switches A and C are closed, only bulbs 1 and 6 will light up. Which of these two bulbs will be the brightest?

a ☐ 6　　b ☐ both the same　　c ☐ 1

3 CIRCUITS

›› SB page 161

Use the clues to do the puzzle and find the key word.

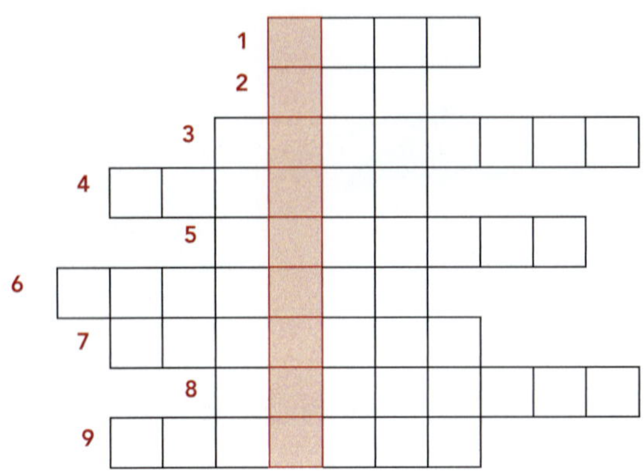

1 unit of voltage
2 unit of resistance in a circuit
3 adjective form of 'electricity'
4 device for enabling current to flow or not
5 instrument for measuring amps
6 device for storing electricity
7 English for *Spannung*
8 Another noun form of 'resistance'
9 this is measured in amps

The key word is ______________________ .

4 AN ACCIDENT REPORT

›› SB page 162

Link the sentence parts to make true statements about Harry Driver's accident.

1 The accident took place in the kitchen	☐	a	and he had to be rushed to hospital.
2 Harry Driver was using an	☐	b	but he could easily have been killed.
3 Harry rested his left hand on a metal	☐	c	earth terminal as it had broken off.
4 An electrical fault in the drill electrified	☐	d	electric drill to drill a hole into a wall.
5 The 3-pin plug of the drill had no	☐	e	kitchen cabinet while he was drilling.
6 The current found its path to earth	☐	f	of a house in Manor Road, Birmingham.
7 Harry was badly hurt by the electric shock	☐	g	the conductive metal parts of the drill.
8 Doctors now say that Harry will recover	☐	h	through Harry's body and the cabinet.

Tools

1 NAMES OF TOOLS

›› SB pages 163–164, exercises 1–2

A Label the tools with a name from the box.

digital multimeter | hex key | mason's hammer | oil can | pipe wrench | pipe bender | pruning shears | smoothing plane | trowel | wire stripper

1 ____________

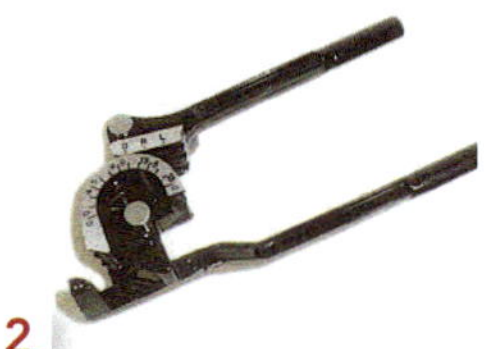
2 ____________

3 ____________

4 ____________

5 ____________

6 ____________

7 ____________

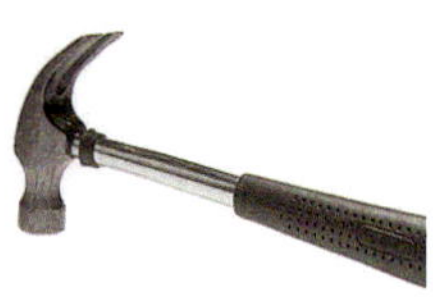
8 ____________

9 ____________

10 ____________

B Complete the table with the English equivalents of the German words.

	German	English
1	*Baumschere*	
2	*Rohrbiegegerät*	
3	*Inbusschlüssel*	
4	*Kelle*	
5	*Abisolierzange*	
6	*Maurerhammer*	
7	*digitales Vielfachmeßgerät*	
8	*Ölkanne*	
9	*Rohrschlüssel*	
10	*Schlichthobel*	

2 WHICH TOOL FOR WHICH JOB?

›› SB pages 163–164

What tool or tools are needed to do the following jobs?

1. to cut a piece of wood in half
2. to cut a copper pipe to length
3. to fit a plug to a 3-core cable
4. to drill a hole into a concrete ceiling
5. to assemble a bookcase from a furniture store
6. to remove the cylinder head from an engine
7. to cut a large branch from a tree easily
8. to make a round chair leg from a square piece of wood
9. to hang a picture on a wall
10. to cut a piece of sheet metal

3 WHICH TOOL FOR WHICH PERSON?

›› SB pages 163–164

First use the words in box A to label the people in the pictures. Be careful: two job descriptions don't fit at all. Then link the tools in box B to the occupations.

A: bricklayer *(Maurer)* | carpenter | dentist | electrician | gardener | mechanic | plumber *(Installateur/in)* | welder

B: chain saw | cold chisel | hacksaw | hex key | insulated *(isoliert)* screwdriver | mason's hammer | multimeter | oil can | pipe bender | pipe wrench | plane | pruning shears | saw | socket wrench | trowel | wire strippers | wood chisel

1

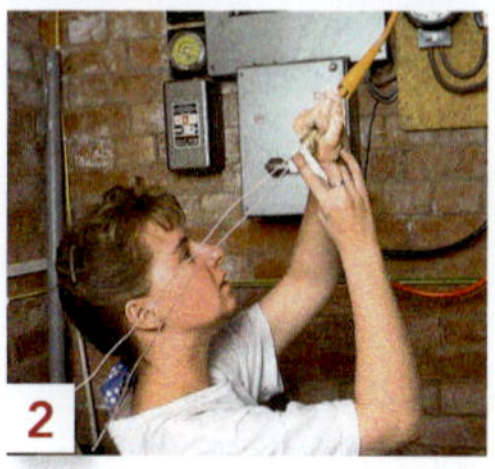
2

3

4

5

6

Materials and their properties

1 OBJECTS AND MATERIALS

›› SB pages 166–167, exercises 1–2

Use a material from box A and the name of an object from box B to label the twelve photos.

A ~~aluminium~~ | brass | cardboard | ceramic | cotton | glass | leather | paper | plastic | rubber | steel | wooden

B bag | beer mug | box | girder | jacket | pallet | petrol can | ~~piston~~ | screw | T-shirt | tyre | windscreen

1 *aluminium piston*

2 ______

3 ______

4 ______

5 ______

6 ______

7 ______

8 ______

9 ______

10 ______

11 ______

12 ______

2 DESCRIBING MATERIALS

›› SB page 167, exercise 3

A Complete the table with the missing words.

	Noun		Adjective	
	English	German	English	German
1	brittleness			
2	conductivity			
3	malleability	*Verformbarkeit*		
4	elasticity			

5 plasticity			
6 porosity			
7 hardness			
8 transparence			

B Complete the sentences with a word or words from the table. Be careful to distinguish between nouns and adjectives.

1 ____________[1] materials like ceramic and cast iron are ____________[2] and strong, but they tend to crack or break on impact.

2 Rubber is the most common ____________ material that is used to make tyres, for example.

3 Silver has a higher ____________[1] than copper, but it is usually too expensive to use as a ____________[2] material in electric circuits.

4 Spring steel *(Federstahl)* has a high ____________ so that it returns to its exact original shape.

5 ____________ can change its shape permanently so it is often used to make the casings of electrical devices.

6 The extreme ____________[1] of plasticine (Knetmasse) makes it wonderful for modelling. Another very ____________[2] material is the clay (Ton).

7 Window glass is the most ____________[1] material but it is also so ____________[2] that it has a very low impact-resistance.

8 A porometer is used to measure the ____________[1] of textiles and other ____________[2] products by measuring the flow of water or air through the material.

3 LOOKING AT THE TEXT

›› SB page 168, text

Link the things 1–10 in the list on the left to a function in list on the right to say what role they play in the text on page 168 of the Student's Book.

1 Gore-Tex	☐	a	trade name of new shock-absorbing material
2 d3o™ Lab	☐	b	European safety standard for motorcycle protection
3 Pro Shell	☐	c	example of garment using new shock-absorbing material
4 EN-1621-1	☐	d	example of high-risk sport
5 TFL Cool System®	☐	e	example of when shock-absorbing material hardens on impact
6 leather glove	☐	f	inventors of a shock-absorbing material that hardens on impact
7 d3o™	☐	g	leather material that protects bikers in all weather conditions
8 slalom racing	☐	h	makers of all-weather protective clothing
9 road accident	☐	i	most important kind of protective clothing for bikers
10 helmet	☐	j	new technology that makes black garments cooler in hot weather

5 Energy

1 ENERGY SOURCES

›› SB pages 170–171

Read the speech bubbles. Which types of energy are the people referring to?

> 1 In Europe, most – almost all – electricity is made by heating water using an unrenewable energy source to produce steam, which then turns a generator. The trouble is, these unrenewable energy sources are likely to run out in the future.

____

> 4 *I know a lot of people think they're ugly and destroy the countryside, but why not build them out at sea?*

____

> 2 *Yes, but isn't it only efficient in sunny places like Spain? I don't think it can produce enough power to help much in northern countries.*

____

> 5 **It may work in places like New Zealand and Iceland where it comes to the surface naturally, but what will happen if we extract it industrially from miles below the earth's cust? Nobody knows.**

____

> 3 Dams are just ugly and they flood beautiful valleys. Just look at what is going on in China. Millions of people have had to leave their homes.

____

> 6 The fact is that these people have already started a very risky, life-threatening *(lebensgefährlich)* process that they can't stop. And now they want to build even more. Are we mad?

____

2 ENERGY CONSUMPTION IN THE USA

›› SB pages 172–173

The pie charts show you where the USA gets its energy from and how it uses it. First, link the three explanatory paragraphs on page 73 (A–C) to the correct pie chart (1–3). Then complete the paragraphs with the missing information.

Source: *US Department of Energy*

1 ☐

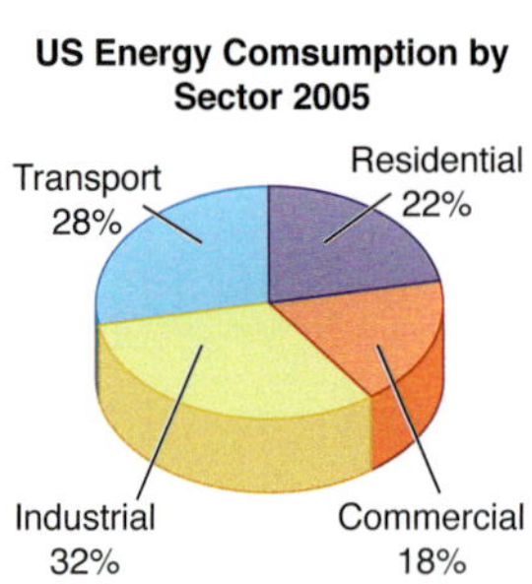

2 ☐

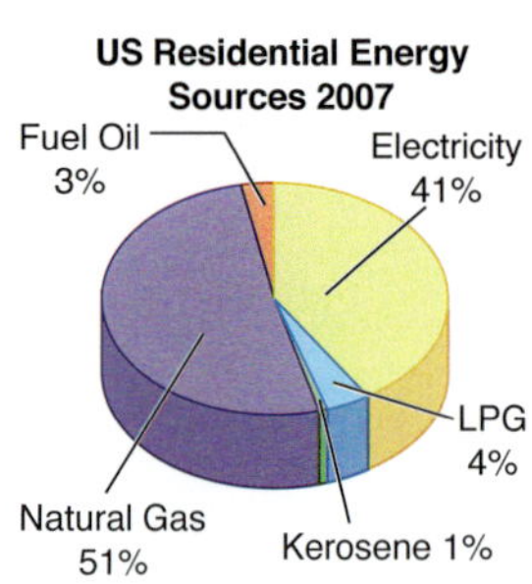

3 ☐

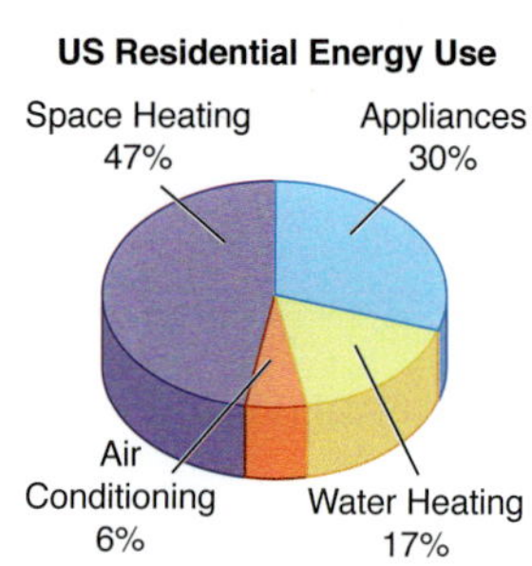

A In ______________[1], Americans obtained the energy they used at home from ______________[2] sources. However, natural gas, which provided ______________[3] of total US residential energy and, at 41 %, ______________[4], were by far the most important. Petroleum products in the form of liquid petrolem gas or "______________"[5] (4 %), fuel oil (3 %) or ______________[6] (1 %) played only a minor role in the mix.

B If we look at how Americans used this ______________[1], we find that by far the most, 47 %, was used for ______________[2], i.e. to heat rooms. The next biggest single use was to power all ______________[3], such as cookers, washers and entertainment equipment (30 %). At ______________[4] and 6 % respectively, remaining ______________[5] was for water heating and ______________[6].

C In ______________[1], energy used in homes was ______________[2] of total US energy consumption, behind ______________[3] with 28 % and ______________[4] uses at 32 %. Commercial uses in stores and offices stood at 18 %, the smallest of the ______________[5] sectors .

3 HOW A HYDROELECTRIC POWER PLANT WORKS

›› SB pages 173–174

A Label the diagram with words/expressions from the text.

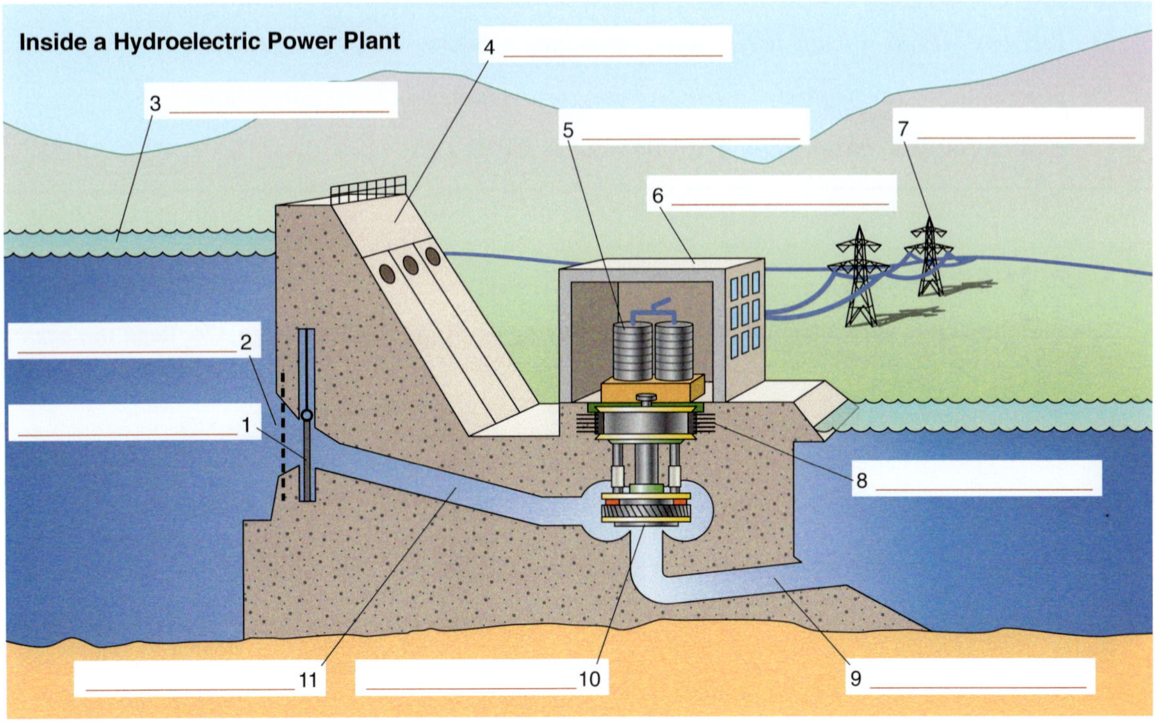

In hydroelectric power plants, water from a reservoir flows under force of gravity through an opening called an intake near the foot of the dam into a sloping penstock *(Druckrohrleitung)*. The volume and speed of the water flow is adjusted by means of a control gate just inside the penstock.

The water flows out of the penstock at the outflow, turning a turbine linked to a generator on its way. Before the current leaves the powerhouse above the turbine and generator, a transformer converts it to a voltage suitable for transmission through power lines.

B Explain how a hydroelectric power plant works *in German*. Use your exercise book.

Safety

1 HAZARDS IN A WORKSHOP

›› SB page 174, exercise 1

Cross out the incorrect prepositions.

Pete Winters, a safety officer, went ~~in~~/into [1] the workshop at/on [2] page 174 to carry on/out [3] a safety check and he wasn't pleased from/with [4] what he saw. Pete looked around/on [5] the room at/in [6] amazement. 'OK,' he said coldly. 'Go in/to [7] the canteen and wait for/on [8] me there.'

Pete began noting down/up [9] everything that went against/around [10] the company's safety rules.

This is what he wrote:

- *open can for/of [11] a toxic substance lying on/in [12] its side; contents running on/on to [13] table*
- *grinder standing at/on [14] floor of/under [15] workbench; cable running diagonally across/on [16] floor*
- *petrol can in/on [17] workbench*
- *tools not at/in [18] tool rack*
- *tool box at/on [19] high shelf with/without [20] means for/of [21] reaching it safely*
- *platform trolley in/on [22] middle from/of [23] room, blocking walkways*
- *tool trolley blocking access into/to [24] emergency exit*

2 SAFETY FIRST

›› SB pages 174–5, exercise 1

Complete the table with information from the drawing on Student's Book page 174. Read the example first.

black/white girl/man | cardboard box | early/later 20s/30s, mid-20s/30s | gloves, goggles, hard hat, safety harness | L-shaped workpiece | short-/long-sleeved shirt/sweatshirt | short/medium-length hair | tower scaffold | welding torch | workbench | (to) do two things at same time | (to) not concentrate on job in hand | (to) lean out too far from sth | (to) not see where one is going | (to) not use/wear protective clothing

Person	Appearance	Activity	Unsafe behaviour
welder	*white girl; early 20s;*	*standing at work-bench;*	*doing two things at the same time;*
window-cleaner			
man in doorway			

3 SIGNS PUZZLE

›› SB page 175, exercise 2; page 176, exercise 4

Use the signs to do the crossword.

Across

1 

3 

5 

8 

9 

Down

1 

2 

4 

6 

7 

4 MEDIATION

Sie möchten jemandem auf Englisch sagen, dass ...

1 ... man in diesem Teil der Fabrik nicht rauchen, essen oder trinken darf.

____

2 ... wegen der Gabelstapler man nur die gelben Laufwege *(walkway)* benutzen sollte.

____

3 ... alle Feuerlöscher einmal im Monat geprüft werden.

____

4 ... Besucher einen Schutzhelm auf der Baustelle tragen müssen.

____

5 ... die meisten Unfälle in Fabriken durch eine Missachtung *(ignoring)* der Sicherheitsvorschriften verursacht werden.

____

____

6 ... Werkzeuge, die nicht mehr gebraucht werden, sofort weggeräumt werden müssen.

____

7 ... Notausgänge stets frei gehalten sein müssen.

____

8 ... alle Unfälle sofort bei der Betriebsleitung gemeldet werden müssen.

____

7 Technical Topics
Supplying the global market

1 LOGISTICS

›› SB page 178, exercise 1

A Give a noun form of the verbs. You'll find them all on page 178 of the Student's Book.

	English	German		English	German
1	haul		7	distribute	
2	manage		8	allocate	
3	supply		9	assemble	
4	inform		10	collect	
5	deliver		11	analyse	
6	use		12	transport	

B Replace the German words or expressions with their English equivalents from the table.

1 Goods ______________________ by land, sea and air. *(befördert werden)*

2 The ______________________ depends on people's qualifications and experience. *(Zuteilung der Arbeit)*

3 Our latest ________________[1] shows that most complaints are about delivery ________________[2]. *(Analyse, Lieferprobleme)*

4 We don't manufacture parts ourselves but ________________[1] parts ________________[2] by others. *(zusammenbauen, geliefert)*

5 Haulage contractors ______________________ goods for their customers. *(abholen und liefern)*

6 It is said that ______________________ is the motor of the new economy. *(Information)*

2 CONTAINERS

›› SB page 178, exercise 2

Complete the captions with a type of packaging from the box.

barrel | bottle | box | can | jar | packet | sack | stick | tub | tube

1 __________ of oil

2 __________ of glue

3 __________ of jam

4 __________ of wine

5 __________ of paint

6 __________ of potatoes

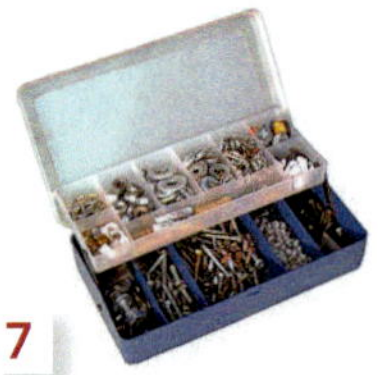

7 __________ of screws

8 __________ of seeds

9 __________ of ice-cream

10 __________ of lipstick

3 A SUPPLY CHAIN

›› SB page 179, exercise 3

A First, look at the jumbled photos of a banana supply chain from the family farm in the Caribbean to the end-consumer in Europe. Then put the photos in the right order from 1–11.

B Give each photo a caption from the box.

Bananas at logistics centre in Europe | Bananas cut off tree | End user/consumer | Fruit on the tree | Loading in Caribbean | Packing in boxes | Point of sale | Transport to Europe by sea | Transport to farm by road | Transport to retailer by road | Washing and labelling

A

B

C

D

E

F

G

H

I

J

K

C Draw a flowchart of the chain of supply.

Fruit on the tree → → → Go on.

8 Technical jobs

1 JOBS

›› SB page 181, exercise 1

Link the jobs in list A to the activities in list B.

A		B
1 carpenter	☐	a changing engine oil
2 electrician	☐	b connecting cooker
3 home entertainment technician	☐	c fitting mechanical-electrical component
4 maintenance technician	☐	d fitting new door
5 mechanic	☐	e fitting a new shower
6 mechatronics technician	☐	f measuring distances on the ground
7 plumber	☐	g connecting a new satellite dish
8 surveying technician	☐	h replacing broken lamp bulb

2 PLACES OF WORK

First label the places of work 1–6 with a word or expression from box A. Then say who works there by choosing the name of a job from box B.

Sort the jobs (box A) and the usual places of work (box B) into the correct column.

A: bicycle repair shop | car repair shop | computer repair shop | electrical workshop | metalworking shop | woodworking shop

B: bicycle mechanic | carpenter | electrician | IT technician | lathe operator | mechanic

1

____

____

2

____

____

3

____

____

4

____

____

5

____

____

6

____

____

3 TALKING ABOUT JOBS

›› SB page 181, exercise 2

Give the word or expression from Student's Book page 181 that fits the definitions.

1 In USA, occasional free day on full pay to do private business that can only be done during working week: ______

2 supplier of electricity, gas and water: ______

3 insurance that pays a capital sum on death or at end of an agreed period: ______

4 everything connected to holding and doing a job, for example, pay, hours of work, overtime, holidays etc: ______

5 internal company fund that provides an additional pension to retired workers: ______

6 insurance that meets medical costs and covers loss of pay when a worker becomes ill: ______

7 adjective used to describe people who work for themselves: ______

8 a smaller sum of money paid during training: ______

4 JOB DESCRIPTIONS

›› SB pages 182–183

Use the elements to complete these sentences from job descriptions and job ads. You must add prepositions and connectors. Be careful about tenses and plural forms.

Example: Carr & Co ... be/construction company/North/England
is a construction company in the North of England.

1 The company is looking ... qualified/electricians/work/its construction site/Berlin

______

2 Successful applicants ... have/minimum/two year's experience/this type/work

______

3 Bonuses ... be paid/good work/in addition/generous salary/help/accommodation ...

______

4 You ... install/complete electrical system/large building/such as/office block

______

5 As a heating technician, ... you/be expected/install/maintain/repair/heating system/office/private home

______

______

6 You ... work/close/architect/site management/achieve/highest standard/work

______

7 Heating technicians and electricians ... must/be able to/work/reliable/own initiative

______

8 Success candidates ... be/good/team worker/who/be able to/cooperate/other

______

9 Low-energy technology

1 SANKEY DIAGRAMS

›› SB page 185, exercise 1

A Link a sentence part from list A to one from list B to make true statements about Sankey diagrams.

A		B
1 In Sankey diagrams, the width of the arrows	☐	a a small energy loss of 5 % in the heating system.
2 Such diagrams are often used	☐	b by the Irish engineer Matthew Sankey in 1898.
3 Sankey diagrams were developed	☐	c caused by extraction, transport and conversion.
4 Sankey's original diagram showed	☐	d energy gains and losses within a building.
5 The Sankey diagram on page 186 illustrates	☐	e is proportionate to quantity or mass.
6 The first arrow shows the loss of primary energy	☐	f the kinetic energy generated by a steam engine.
7 The first arrow at the bottom shows	☐	g solar energy amount to some 79.6 %.
8 According to the diagram, the gains of	☐	h to show the useful energy or efficiency of machines.

B Answer these questions on the Sankey diagram on page 185 of the Student's Book.

1 How much of the energy input is converted into heat energy?

a ☐ 24 % b ☐ 30 % c ☐ 46 % d ☐ 70 %

2 How much heat energy is lost through open doors and windows?

a ☐ 18 % b ☐ 24 % c ☐ 40 % d ☐ 70 %

3 How much heat energy is not lost through the roof and the floor?

a ☐ 6 % b ☐ 8 % c ☐ 56 % d ☐ 62 %

4 If the roof and floor were completely insulated, i. e. zero heat loss, how much energy would be saved?

a ☐ 14 % b ☐ 28 % c ☐ 46 % d ☐ 70 %

2 AN ECO-HOUSE

›› SB page 186, exercise 2

Complete this description of the eco-house on page 186 of the Student's Book.

The drawing is of an ______________ [1] as seen from the front. The house has ______________ [2] floors and a roof space. We can see four ______________ [3] at the front which have ______________ [4]. The outer ______________ [5] and ______________ [6] are fitted with ______________ [7] – shown in red – to stop heat loss. On the roof, there are ______________ [8] and photovoltaic cells to collect heat energy from the ______________ [9] as well as a ______________ [10] to generate ______________ [11]. To the right of the house there is a ______________ [12] that is served by ______________ [13] heat energy. Finally, we can see a row of ______________ [14] to the left of the house.

3 CONDENSING BOILERS

›› SB page 187, exercise 3

Read the text on condensing boilers on page 187 of the Student's Book to complete the sentences with the English equivalents of the German words and expressions. They are in the same order. Be careful about plural forms.

1 Do ______________________________ really pay for themselves quite quickly? *Brennwertkessel*

2 A ______________________________ transfers heat from one medium into another. *Wärmetauscher*

3 Non-condensing boilers waste the heat from ______________________________. *Verbrennungsgase*

4 Condensing boilers save energy by ______________________________ water. *anheizen*

5 The combustion process in the boiler produces excess ______________________________. *Wasserdampf*

6 The condensate from the boiler is led away through a ______________________________. *Abflußrohr*

7 The ______________________________ of condensing boilers is over 90 %. *energetischer Wirkungsgrad*

8 ______________________________ are likely to continue to increase steeply. *Energiekosten*

4 A SOLAR WATER HEATER

›› SB page 187, exercise 3

A Match the words and expressions with the numbers on the drawing.

A solar water heater makes use of the physical principle that hot water rises and cold water sinks. The diagram on the right shows how this works in a domestic water heating system.

- ☐ cold water at bottom of tank
- ☐ cold water reheated in solar collector
- ☐ cold water returns to solar collector
- ☐ hot water at top of tank
- ☐ hot water rises to tank
- ☐ insulation
- ☐ tank

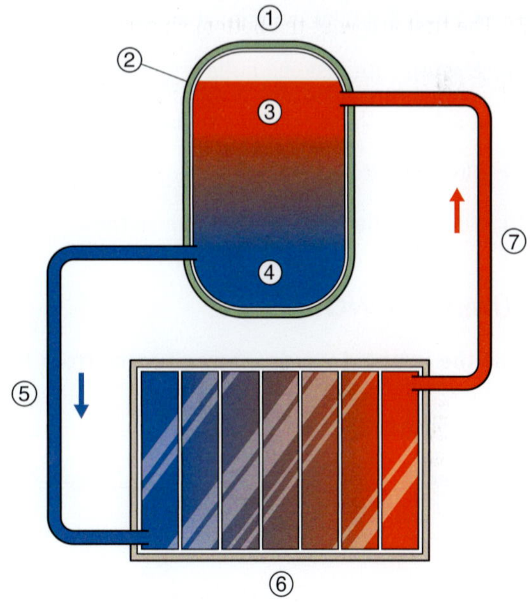

B Use the labels and the material below to write a description of how a solar water heater works.

(to) be made up/consist of | (to) be heated by the sun | (to) heat up/cool down and rise/sink | (to) be pushed up into | (to) sink down into | (to) enter/leave the tank/solar collector | (to) collect at the top/bottom of the tank/solar collector | (to) pass through a pipe to ... | (to) be insulated | (to) continue throughout the day

____

____

____

____

____

____

____

10 Easing the load

1 FORCE-DISTANCE SUBSTITUTION

›› SB page 189, exercise 2

Complete the sentences with a part from the box to make correct statements.

a fixed point such as a beam | are used to raise and lower elevators | does not reduce the required force at all | force by a factor of 4 | much bigger sailing boats possible | number of separate pulleys required | the less the force, the longer the rope | to the weight, the other end is pulled | ~~was first described by Archimedes~~ | 'work energy' needed to do a job

1 The principle of force-distance substitution *was first described by Archimedes.*
2 'Force-distance substitution' reduces the ______
3 In a block & pulley setup, ______
4 One end of the rope is attached to ______
5 The invention of the block & pulley made ______
6 A block & pulley setup must be attached to ______
7 A setup with just one pulley ______
8 A setup with four pulleys reduces the ______
9 Block & pulley systems ______
10 Double pulleys are used to reduce the ______

2 JUMBLED WORDS

›› SB pages 189–190

Sort the jumbled words. They all come from the texts on page 189 and 190 of the Student's Book.

1 A **draluyich** ______[1] system is filled with a **quilid** ______[2], most commonly a thin **ilo** ______[3], that moves the pistons within the cylinders.

2 In a hydraulic system, the **crofe** ______[1] that is required to move the piston in the smaller **linceryd** ______[2] is multiplied to move a greater **dalo** ______[3] with the other piston.

3 To calculate the mechanical **gaatvaned** ______[1] of a given system, all you have to do is **iddive** ______[2] the area of the larger **topins edah** ______[3] by the area of the smaller one.

4 Because of the principle of force-distance **tottissubuni** ______[1], in a system with a mechanical advantage of 4, say, the piston in the smaller cylinder has to **vlater** ______[2] four times further than the piston in the **graler** ______[3] cylinder.

3 ADVERBS AND PREPOSITIONS

Put in the missing prepositions or adverbs from the box.

as | between | by (x3) | from | in (x4) | into (x2) | of (x5) | out of | through | upwards | with | within

___[1] a block & pulley setup ___[2] two pulleys, the weight ___[3] the load is divided evenly ___[4] them. The means that ___[5] such setups a weight ___[6], say, 30 kg can be moved ___[7] a force ___[8] 15 kg. However, the rope or cable ___[9] which the weight is suspended has to travel twice ___[10] far. That is what is meant ___[11] "force-distance substitution", which translates the amount ___[12] work required ___[13] distance.

The same mechanical principle is applied ___[14] hydraulic systems ___[15] which the rope ___[16] a block and pulley setup is represented ___[17] a piston ___[18] a cylinder. When hydraulic oil is pumped ___[19] the cylinder, the piston moves ___[20] it; when the oil is taken out ___[21] the cylinder, the piston moves ___[22] it.

4 PASSIVE

Complete the sentences with the passive form of the verbs.

1 Engines ___ (usually + lift) out of cars with the help of a block and pulley setup.

2 In a setup with two pulleys, the load ___[1] (divide) between them, thus halving the amount of upward force that ___[2] (must apply) in order to lift it.

3 The principle of force-distance substitution means that the force that ___[1] (have to exert) on a load ___[2] (can reduce), but the distance that ___[3] (have to travel) ___[4] (increase) by a corresponding amount.

4 In photo 4 on page 188, earth ___[1] (load) on to a truck by a machine that ___[2] (call) an 'earth mover'.

5 Elevators in buildings ___[1] (raise and lower) by means of a complex block and pulley setup that ___[2] (power) by electric motors.

6 In the drawing on page 190, a force of 10N ___[1] (translate) into one of 30N. The mechanical advantage can ___[2] (easily calculate) if the area of the larger piston head ___[3] (divide) by the area of the smaller one.

11 Data collection and storage

1 SOLID STATE STORAGE

›› SB page 191, exercise 1

Link a component or technical concept in list A with its function or definition in list B.

A			B
1	cell sensor	a	cell at intersections of grid in a flash memory
2	fifty-percent threshold	b	data storage device
3	flash memory	c	electronic component without any moving parts
4	Fowler-Nordheim tunneling	d	limit that determines if a value is 0 or 1
5	oxide layer	e	measures the charge passing through the floating gate
6	solid-state	f	range of electrical charge in a flash memory
7	10–13 volts	g	separates the two transistors in a flash memory
8	two-transistor cell	h	technique for altering the position of electrons in a flash memory

2 LETTER TO THE EDITOR

›› SB page 192, exercise 2

A Complete the table with a synonym from the text for the words or expressions in the list. They are all in paragraphs 1–6 of page 192 in the Student's Book, but they are not necessarily in the same order.

	Word/expression	Synonym in text
1	bought and sold	
2	collected	
3	construct	
4	forecast	
5	huge quantities	
6	in my opinion	
7	interaction with others	
8	invisible	
9	separated out	
10	overpowering	
11	tried out	
12	possibilities for misuse	

B Find the English equivalents of the German words or expressions in the table in exercise 2A.

1 *unsichtbar* ______________________

2 *nicht nachweisbar* ______________________

3 *vorhersagen* (2 meanings) ______________________

4 *Handel treiben* (2 meanings) ______________________

5 *soziale Interaktion* ______________________

6 *riesige Mengen* (2 meanings) ______________________

7 *meiner Meinung nach* (2 meanings) ______________________

8 *speichern* ______________________

9 *Missbrauch* ______________________

10 *zügeln* ______________________

3 QUESTIONS ON THE LETTER

›› SB page 192, exercise 2

Answer the questions.

1 Describe how governments and companies treat people's personal data.

____

____

2 Point out in what circumstances the collection, storage and processing of personal data need not necessarily be particularly dangerous.

____

____

3 List the ways in which Big Brother is watching YOU.

____

____

____

4 Say why Britain's National Identity Register is 'highly controversial'.

____

____

4 COLLECTING DATA

›› SB page 193, exercise 3

Which devices are used mainly for ...

1 ... surveillance? ______________________

2 ... establishing identity? ______________________

3 ... communication? ______________________

4 ... data storage? ______________________

5 ... self-service? ______________________

12 Technical Topics
Robotics

1 INDUSTRIAL ROBOTS

›› SB page 194 exercise 1

Cross out the incorrect prepositions or particles.

1 A robotic arm is made up in/up of of joints called 'axes'.
2 If you go in/into [1] a car assembly plant, you'll see that many machines are fitted on to/with [2] robotic arms.
3 The 'hand' is a tool like a paint gun or wrench fixed in/to [1] the end from/of [2] the arm.
4 The final axis at/of [1] a robotic arm is equivalent to/with [2] the human wrist but it can revolve round/through [3] 360° in/of [4] each direction.
5 Although industrial robots are similar in/to [1] human arms, humanoid robots are actually built in/on [2] the shape from/of [3] humans.
6 Humanoids are different from/in [1] industrial robots at/in [2] so far as they can move around/in [3] a space.

2 HUMANOID ROBOTS

›› SB pages 194–5, exercises 2–3

A Label the robot's axes with the equivalent human joints.

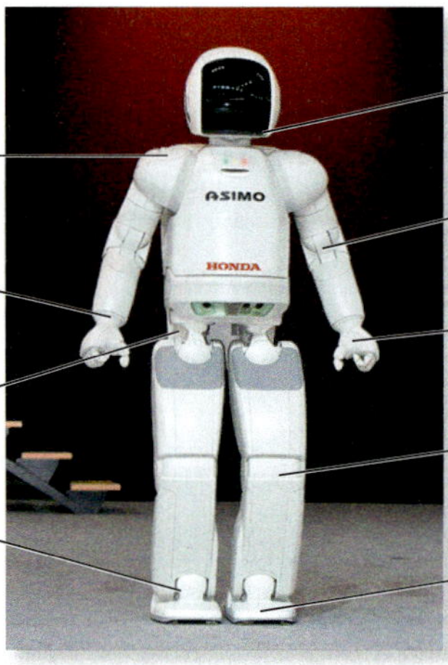

1 Nacken *neck*
2 Schulter ____________
3 Ellenbogen ____________
4 Handgelenk ____________
5 Hand ____________
6 Hüfte ____________
7 Knie ____________
8 Sprunggelenk ____________
9 Fuß ____________

B Which joints or 'axes' would the robot use to perform the tasks below?

1 Go up stairs. To go up stairs, the robot would use his ____
____.
2 Open a door. To open a door, he'd ____
____.
3 Bend down. To bend down, ____
____.
4 File a piece of steel. ____
____.
5 Saw a length of wood in half. ____
____.
6 Walk across a room. ____
____.

3 ROBOTIC BASICS

›› SB page 195, exercise 3

Tick (✓) the correct alternative.

1 Basic robots consist of ... main sub-assemblies.

a ☐ two b ☐ three c ☐ four

2 These robots have ... axes.

a ☐ four b ☐ five c ☐ six

3 The ... is the area a robot can work in.

a ☐ area of working b ☐ working envelope c ☐ working area

4 Robots are powered by ...

a ☐ air pressure b ☐ electricity c ☐ magnetism.

5 Axis 3 and 4 are equivalent to a human's ...

a ☐ elbow and forearm b ☐ elbow and wrist c ☐ forearm and wrist.

6 Output gives the computer the robot's exact ...

a ☐ activity b ☐ position c ☐ speed.

7 The computer is programmed by means of a ...

a ☐ remote control b ☐ teach handset c ☐ teach pendant.

8 A robot's movement can be as fast as ... metres per second.

a ☐ 1.5 b ☐ 2 c ☐ 2.5

4 WORD SNAKE

Split the word snake into its component words and insert the missing punctuation and capital letters. There are two sentences.

accordingtostatisticsissuedbytheusdepartmentoflaborincreasedautomationmost importantlythegrowinguseofindustrialrobotshascausedthehugemajorityofjobloss esinAmericanmanufacturingindustriesoverthelasttwentyyearsorsoinspiteofmedia hysteriaaboutjobsmovingtoasiaandeasterneuropeinfactjobmigrationhasplayedam uchsmallerrolethanusuallythought

Focus on Success – The new edition: Ausgabe Technik Workbook
wurde geplant und entwickelt von Cornelsen Berufliche Bildung, Berlin.

Verfasser: David Clarke, Witten
Michael Macfarlane, Oxford

Projektleitung: Jim Austin
Verlagsredaktion: Andreas Goebel
Außenredaktion: James Abram
Bildredaktion: Gertha Maly
Layout und technische Umsetzung: sign, Berlin
Umschlaggestaltung: werkstatt für gebrauchsgrafik, Berlin

Illustrationen: Oxford Designers & Illustrators
Bildquellen: Cover: Fotofinder: A1PIX; DLR; istockphoto; Fotofinder: Karlheinz Oster
RF photos: Alamy: S. 7/O. Dimier, S. 14/1/Alvery&Towers Picture Library, S. 14/4, S. 14/7/Somos Group, S. 24/Image Source Pink, S. 25/Dynamic Graphics, S. 38/Comstock, S. 44, S. 49/B2M Productions, S. 57/1/2 Aardvark, S. 69/4/moodboard; Istockphoto: S. 77/1/2/10/11; V. Maly: S. 76/8/9; Shutterstock: S. 10, S. 14/2, S. 14/3, S. 14/5, S. 23, S. 36, S. 68, S. 70, S. 76, S. 78
RM photos: Alamy: S. 12/J. Wiedel, S. 21/S. Kiefer, S. 50/T. Koene, S. 52/J. Morgan, S. 56/H. Barlow; S. 69/1/P. Dunn; S. 69/2/M. Jenkinson, S. 69/3/D. Williams; Cinetext: S. 27; Fotofinder: S. 11/Bildagentur-online, S. 16/photoplexus, S. 20/Visum/J. Rezac, S. 46/ImageSource, S. 69/5/J. Eckel, S. 69/6/J. Lantelme; S. 77/4/Visum/PanosPicture, S. 77/5/Eye Ubiquitous/Hutchison, S. 77/6/Joker/A. Lubitz, S. 77/7/Visum/K.Singer, S. 77/8/Thomas Callsen, S. 77/9/Karlheinz Oster, S. 78/1/allOver Bildagentur, S. 78/2/Gottfried Stoppel, S. 78/3/Andreas Buck, S. 78/4/Variopress, S. 78/5/Variopress, S. 78/6/Bilderbox; Gettyimages: S. 14/6/P. Adams, S. 14/8/AltrendoImages; UllsteinBild: S. 77/3/KPA, S. 83

Cartoons: S. 31/CartoonStock

Mit freundlicher Unterstützung: www.fluid-online.de/S68/2

www.cornelsen.de

1. Auflage, 2. Druck 2011

Alle Drucke dieser Auflage sind inhaltlich unverändert und können im Unterricht nebeneinander verwendet werden.

Druck: Himmer AG, Augsburg

ISBN 978-3-06-020270-6

Inhalt gedruckt auf säurefreiem Papier aus nachhaltiger Forstwirtschaft.

Refresher Course

A FREE-TIME ACTIVITIES

1 Free-time activities

1 fishing
2 (horse) riding
3 reading
4 playing online poker
5 clubbing
6 making/mixing music

2 Prepositions

1 in front of	5 round	9 off
2 about	6 against	10 for
3 out	7 in	11 with
4 around	8 at	12 out of

3 Subject and object pronouns

1 ¹ you, ² I, ³ you
2 ¹ you, ² I, ³ him, ⁴ he
3 ¹ It, ² it, ³ them
4 ¹ I, ² them, ³ we, ⁴ them
5 ¹ It, ² me, ³ they, ⁴ her
6 ¹ She, ² him, ³ he

4 Simple present

1 Dana does voluntary work (on) three evenings a week.
2 Ravi is in a football club and he plays in/for the first team.
3 Ravi and Jack enjoy clubbing but they don't go very often.
4 How often does Lucy go to work each week?
5 Sal and Sam don't play violent games. They prefer to test their skill.
6 Do you have a lot of free time or do you work?

5 Present progressive

A man is buying an ice cream at the kiosk. A boy and girl are sunbathing on a red blanket. A family is having a picnic under a tree. A girl is talking on a mobile phone. Two boys are jumping near some steps. A bird is standing on a bistro table. A girl is diving from a diving board. A man in blue boxer shorts is having a shower. A girl is reading on a red sunlounger. A woman is climbing out of the pool.

6 Simple present or present progressive?

1 go	6 don't like
2 often reads	7 Are you planning?
3 is having	8 do you drink
4 ¹ always do, ² get	9 is coming out.
5 Do you sometimes eat	10 prefers

7 Simple present or present progressive?

1 ¹ spends, ² is working, ³ doesn't think, ⁴ is enjoying / enjoys
2 ¹ works, ² is doing ³ enjoys
3 ¹ has, ² doesn't play / isn't playing, ³ hangs / is hanging

8 Worldfield: free-time activities

(freie Lösung)

B GIRLS FIGHT FOR THEIR RIGHTS

1 Questions and answers

1 f	3 c	5 b	7 e
2 g	4 h	6 d	8 a

2 Word search

1 teammate	6 win
2 compete	7 wrestle
3 fan	8 training
4 sports	9 volleyball
5 rival	10 winner

3 The simple past

1 trained	5 bought
2 won	6 chose
3 came	7 took
4 wore	8 arrived

4 Negatives in the simple past

1 didn't watch TV – watched a DVD
2 didn't go – went
3 didn't have a burger – She had chicken
4 didn't take a bus – They took a train
5 didn't play golf – We played tennis
6 didn't score any goals – scored two
7 didn't meet Lucy – He met Sandra
8 didn't buy – I bought

5 Asking questions about the past

1 When did Josh and Janna go bowling?
2 Why did they miss their booking?
3 How long did they wait for a free lane?
4 When did they finally start their first game?
5 Why did they become angry?
6 Who did Josh complain to about the faulty lane?
7 What was the problem (with this)?
8 When did Josh and Janna finally arrive home?

C YOU ARE WHAT YOU EAT

1 In a restaurant

1 c	3 f	5 b	7 h
2 d	4 a	6 e	8 g

2 Odd word out

1 The odd word out is 'scampi' because this is a fish, not meat.
2 The odd word out is 'beer' because this is an alcoholic drink and the other three are non-alcoholic or soft drinks.
3 The odd word out is 'carrots', because this is a vegetable and the other three are fruit.
4 The odd word out is 'peanuts', because it is the only food which has nuts in it. The other three are potato products.
5 The odd word out is 'prawn cocktail', because this is a starter and the other three are desserts.

3 Possessive adjectives

1 My	3 Her	5 Its	7 our
2 His	4 their	6 your	

4 Countable and uncountable nouns

1 x
2 [1] a, [2] a/the, [3] a/the
3 [1] x, [2] x, [3] x
4 [1] x, [2] x, [3] x, [4] x
5 [1] a, [2] a
6 a

5 Uncountable nouns

a *bit/piece* of cheese
two *bars* of chocolate
a *bottle* of ketchup
three *jars* of jam
two *loaves* of bread
a *packet* of butter
six *rolls* of toilet paper
two *cans* of peas
a large *tub* of ice cream
a *tube* of toothpaste

6 Uncountable nouns and singular verbs

1 evidence shows
2 information comes
3 advice is
4 research proves
5 software costs
6 furniture ... looks

7 Some, any

1 [1] some, [2] any
2 [1] some, [2] some
3 [1] any, [2] some, [3] some
4 [1] any, [2] some

8 Something/anything, ...

1 anything
2 [1] somewhere, [2] anywhere
3 [1] something, [2] anything, [3] somewhere
4 anything
5 [1] somebody, [2] anything
6 [1] somewhere, [2] somebody, [3] anything/(something)

9 Much, many, a lot of/plenty of

1 much
2 much
3 a lot of
4 [1] many, [2] plenty of
5 many
6 [1] plenty of, [2] many

10 (A) little, (a) few

1 a little
2 little
3 [1] few, [2] a few
4 [1] few, [2] a little
5 a little
6 [1] little, [2] a little

D TIME OUT

1 Working with words

1 details
2 exciting place
3 are against
4 sad
5 attitude to
6 thinks
7 chance
8 go to
9 agrees with her parents
10 points out
11 planning to get a job
12 sensible

2 The *will* future

1 [1] won't rain, [2] will be
2 Will you help
3 [1] 'll miss, [2] 'll be
4 [1] won't forget, [2] 'll call, [3] won't need
5 will your flight take
6 'll never lend

3 The *going to* future

1 are going to visit
2 'm going to arrange
3 Are you going to work
4 [1] aren't going to take, [2] 're going to have to start
5 Is Holly going to have
6 's going to take off

4 Which future form?

1 Are you going to go
2 Is Holly really going to take
3 [1] 'll be, [2] 'll have to start
4 'll see
5 'll finish
6 are going to stop

5 Present progressive with future meaning

1	are you doing	7	not doing
2	'm going	8	'm staying
3	Are you going	9	are visiting
4	are coming	10	'm not going
5	is meeting	11	'm spending
6	Are you doing		

6 Train times

1 leave - leaves - 6:00
2 does the last train from Paris - last train from Paris arrives
3 does the train stop - Saarbrücken, Kaisers-lautern and Mannheim
4 does the journey take - takes three hours and 53 minutes

E SHOPPING

1 Puzzle

1	staff	7	money
2	Armani	8	bargain
3	pushy	9	label
4	clothes	10	silk
5	online	11	queue
6	store		

The keyword is 'fashionable'.

2 Adjectives

1	foolish	7	public
2	honest	8	painful
3	furious	9	naughty
4	angry	10	crazy
5	harmless	11	full
6	new	12	furious

3 Adverbs

1 well
2 dances wonderfully
3 runs fast
4 drives carefully
5 unexpectedly
6 people work hard
7 paints skilfully
8 dances badly

4 When to use adjectives and adverbs

1 c	3 e	5 d
2 a	4 f	6 b

5 Translation

1 terrible - terribly tired.
2 usually has a quiet life - she had an unusual experience.
3 suddenly heard - sudden noise woke him up
4 The music was so loud - had to talk to one another very loudly

F READY FOR A JOB?

1 Photos

1 5c	3 -	5 1a	7 6a
2 3b	4 4a	6 1c	8 2c

2 Jobs

indoor job	usual place of work	outdoor job	usual place of work
baby-sitter	private home	building worker	building site
waiter	restaurant	car-washer	garage
cashier	shop, self-service store	courier rider	street
shop assistant	shop, self-service store	delivery boy/girl	street
kitchen help	restaurant	dog-exerciser	street, local park, garden
shelf filler	shop, self-service store	gardener	garden, local park

3 Present perfect

1 [1] heard, [2] bought	4 has ... had
2 switched	5 [1] has left, [2] (has) got
3 has ... known	6 have ... started

4 For, since

1 for	4 for	7 for
2 since	5 for	8 for
3 since	6 since	

5 There's still work to do

1 haven't done ... yet.
2 still haven't cleaned
3 haven't fed ... yet
4 still hasn't cut
5 hasn't washed his ... yet
6 still hasn't done

6 Spot the mistake

1 've lived	5 Have you seen
2 went	6 hasn't phoned
3 've finished	7 haven't spoken
4 cut	8 has told

7 Translation

1 has bought a new guitar
2 have lived in Germany for five years
3 Have you seen the ... film?
4 haven't visited my grandparents since Christmas

Main Course

1 CITY LIGHTS

1 Prepositions

1 in	6 on	11 up	16 by
2 in	7 of	12 over	17 on
3 to	8 near	13 from	18 at
4 with	9 at	14 about	19 at
5 at	10 on	15 on	20 to

2 Building skills: using your own words

A

Verb	Noun
breathe	breath
explore	exploration
construct	construction
fail	failure
recover	recovery

Noun	Adjective
distance	distant
tradition	traditional
energy	energetic
technology	technological
freedom	free

B

1 tradition
2 construction of skyscrapers
3 a failure to control drugs and crime (in New York)
4 recovery took quite a long time
5 the freedom to start again

3 Comparison of adjectives

A

1 the most expensive	5 lighter
2 the most economical	6 the safest
3 as powerful as	7 the most comfortable
4 faster	

B

1 the cheapest	5 the slowest
2 as economical as	6 the least powerful
3 the lightest	7 the least comfortable
4 the most dangerous	

4 Too ... and (not) ... enough

Mother: Listen, that car is too old to drive across America.
Father: Yes, the car isn't tough enough to go all that way.
Mother: I agree: it isn't reliable enough for such a big trip.
Father: I really think Oregon is too far away for this old vehicle – and for you.
Mother: Yes, you're too young for something like this.
Father: Yes, you're not / aren't experienced enough for a journey across the USA.
Mother: And think about the cost of fuel: it is too expensive now.
Father: Yes, ancient cars like this one aren't economical enough.

5 Problems with comparison

1 ~~as~~ = than
2 ~~of~~ = in
3 ~~famousest~~ = most famous
4 ~~like~~ = as
5 ~~so~~ = as
6 ~~like~~ = as
7 ~~more old~~ = older

6 Wordfield: city life

A *(siehe Seite 19)*

B

1 capital
2 boroughs
3 [1] Building, [2] skyscrapers
4 attraction
5 [1] crowded, [2] traffic
6 community

7 Technical options

1 Accidents and bad weather are frequent causes of long tailbacks on freeways.
2 A traffic flow system can only work if all drivers keep to the recommended speed.
3 In this system, traffic density is measured by loop detectors beneath the surface of the road.
4 When the tailback breaks up, the control system deactivates automatically.

2 ADVERTISING

1 Opposites

A

1 future (line 3)	5 growing (line 34)
2 online (line 8)	6 beginning (line 37)
3 simple (line 15)	7 including (line 39)
4 someone (line 27)	8 together (line 43)

B

1 [1] online, [2] offline
2 [1] shrinking, [2] growing
3 [1] no-one, [2] someone
4 [1] including, [2] excluding

2 Past progressive and simple past

1 The sun was rising when Mandy got a taxi to the airport.
2 Everything was going well, when they suddenly had a puncture.
3 She looked at her watch while the taxi driver was changing the wheel. She was going to be late!
4 When they started again the roads were getting very busy with the morning rush hour.
5 They were calling her flight for the last time when she finally checked in.
6 While she was running to the gate she saw her friend Alice by the gate and waved.
7 She was still explaining her terrible journey when they got on the plane.
8 And that was not the end of it! They flew into a terrible storm while they were coming down to land in Ibiza.
9 While they were waiting for a bus to their hotel they got wet and cold in the rain.
10 But thank goodness! The sun came out while they were driving to the hotel.

3 Relative clauses and contact clauses

1 who/that	6 who/that	11 which/that
2 X	7 who/that	12 X
3 X	8 X	13 X
4 X	9 X	14 which/that
5 X	10 which/that	

4 Building skills: analyzing charts

A Japan
B There was a steady rise in GDP from 2002-2004. After that, it declined from 2004-2006. Then it stayed the same in 2006-7 before a big increase in 2008.
C In Germany GDP decreased slightly from 1996-1998. In 1998 it remained flat before going down again until 2000. GDP increased sharply from 2002.

5 Wordfield: advertising

Across

7 advertising	16 designer	18 clients
15 contract	17 planner	

Down

1 choice	6 campaign	12 creative
2 images	8 technique	13 sales
3 leaflets	9 brochure	14 spend
4 product	10 chart	
5 branded	11 costs	

6 Technical options

A

1 strip lighting	3 halogen bulb
2 Edison bulb	4 CFL

B

1 support wires	6 wire conductors
2 argon	7 outer screw thread contact
3 tungsten filament	8 insulation
4 glass bulb	9 inner electrical foot contact
5 glass mount	

3 MEDIA MADNESS

1 Modal verbs

A

1 ought to / could
2 should / ought to
3 could / can
4 should / ought to
5 shouldn't / can't
6 can

B

1 needn't
2 must
3 needn't
4 mustn't
5 mustn't
6 must

C *(freie Lösung)*

2 Modal verb substitutes

A

1 d
2 c
3 b
4 a

B

1 had to
2 wasn't allowed to
3 had to
4 was allowed to
5 wasn't able to
6 had to
7 was able to
8 didn't have to

C

1 wasn't able to
2 'm not allowed
3 'll have to
4 didn't have to
5 was able to
6 won't be able to
7 'll have to

3 Problems with modal verbs

1 ~~can~~ = can speak
2 ~~mustn't~~ = needn't
3 ~~must~~ = had to
4 ~~Do you can~~ = Can you
5 ~~You don't mustn't~~ = You mustn't
6 ~~will~~ = wants
7 ~~would~~ = want

4 Building skills: mediation

(Lösungsvorschlag) Englisch-Muttersprachler sind bemüht, in einem Gespräch von Angesicht zu Angesicht höflich zu klingen/sein. Dies ist in einer Online-Diskussion genau so wichtig. Die meisten (Internet-)Foren haben ihre eigenen Regeln, aber hier sind ein paar allgemeine Hinweise, wie man sich in einem Internet-Forum verhalten soll.

- Bleiben Sie beim Thema – schreiben Sie nur über das Thema, über das gerade diskutiert wird.
- Schreiben Sie nicht alles in BLOCKSCHRIFT. Dies wird als „Schreien" betrachtet und ist (außerdem) schlecht lesbar. Wenn Sie etwas hervorheben wollen, benutzen Sie **Fettschrift** oder <u>unterstreichen</u> Sie es.
- Benutzen Sie Anfangsgroßbuchstaben für Namen, Orte usw. – ansonsten machen Sie einen faulen/nachlässigen Eindruck.
- Überprüfen Sie Ihre Rechtschreibung und Grammatik und vermeiden Sie zu viele Abkürzungen, da andere (Leser) sie vielleicht nicht verstehen.
- Seien Sie den anderen Nutzern gegenüber höflich und respektieren Sie sie und ihre Ideen.
- Verwenden Sie normale Satzzeichen – es ist nicht nötig „!!!!" oder „????" zu schreiben, um einen Punkt zu untermauern/zu unterstreichen.

5 Wordfield: the media

A *(siehe Seite 19)*

B

1 reality
2 texting
3 audience
4 viewer
5 comedy
6 press
7 blog
8 documentary

6 Technical options

1 front panel
2 on/off
3 open/close
4 headphones
5 volume
6 display
7 disc tray
8 chapter
9 time elapsed
10 pause
11 stop
12 chapter skip

4 ON THE MOVE

1 *If*-sentences type I

1 *Steve:* Listen. If we go west, we'll get to Dustville. And if we go there, we'll be able to go to the concert in the park.
Carrie: Yes, but we'll have to ride through the noisy, dirty city if we do that.
2 *Carrie:* Now look, if we go north, we'll get up into the mountains. And if we go there, we'll have some excellent views.
Steve: Yes, but we'll have to climb lots of steep hills if we do that.
3 *Steve:* What about this idea? If we get down to the beach, we'll be able to go for a swim.
Carrie: Yes, but we'll get sand in all our clothes if we do that.
4 *Carrie:* What about another idea? If we get into the forest, we can have a picnic by the river.
Steve: Yes, but we might get lost in the forest if we do that.

2 *If*-sentences type 2

1 If I was hot and wanted to go swimming, I would get/go down to the beach.
2 If my gears were broken, I would go to Dustville to look for a bike shop.
3 If I wanted some photos of beautiful views across the country, I would get / go up into the mountains.
4 If I was tired and wanted to have a sleep somewhere cool and quiet, I would camp by / go to the river in the forest.

3 *If*-sentences types 1 and 2

2 If we miss that bus, another one will soon come and we'll be able to catch that.
3 If one of us moved, we could be together all the time.
4 If I had enough money, I would buy a car, and then I would be able to visit more often.
5 You'll save money on petrol if you choose a / the smaller one.
6 If everybody bought smaller cars, it would be better for the environment.

4 Word families

A

Verb	Noun	Adjective *-ing* form	Adjective *-ed* form
pollute	*pollution*	*polluting*	polluted
damage	*damage*	damaging	*damaged*
exhaust	*exhaustion*	*exhausting*	*exhausted*
improve	improvement	*improving*	improved
increase	increase	increasing	*increased*

B

2 [1] polluted/damaged, [2] pollution/damage
3 [1] pollution, [2] polluting
4 [1] improving, [2] improvements
5 [1] exhausting, [2] exhausted

5 Worldfield: transport

1 taxes
2 route
3 tailback
4 congested
5 passengers
6 expensive
7 commuter
8 range
9 truck
10 transport

6 Building skills: describing and commenting on cartoons

(Lösungsvorschläge)

1 (D) This cartoon shows a station with a lot of passengers who are waiting for a train.
2 (D) Near us we see a female passenger who looks amazed / shocked / surprised and anxious / worried as she reads a sign which directs here to a waiting (& waiting & waiting) room.
3 (A) The cartoon suggests that trains are often late and unreliable.
4 (A) It also shows that passengers are helpless and cannot do anything to make the trains run on time / faster / cannot do anything to complain.
5 (C) The cartoonist may be right about the trains in Britain and America.
6 (C) However, in my opinion it isn't fair to attack the German trains in this way since they usually run on time / punctually / they are usually very reliable.

7 Technical options

1 aerial
2 roof
3 driver's door
4 windscreen
5 wing mirror
6 bonnet
7 numberplate
8 front grill
9 headlight
10 bumper
11 wing
12 side window
13 tyre
14 wheel
15 rear light

5 GREEN ENOUGH?

1 Word pairs

A

1 Revolution
2 change
3 levels
4 fuels
5 emissions
6 power
7 fusion
8 warming

B

1 sea levels
2 global warming
3 Industrial Revolution
4 climate change
5 CO_2 emissions
6 solar power
7 fossil fuels
8 nuclear fission

2 Past perfect

1 realized
2 had been
3 had arrived
4 saw
5 thought
6 had left
7 had killed
8 tried
9 shot
10 remembered
11 had fallen
12 had broken
13 froze
14 had fallen
15 heard
16 had learned
17 started
18 had found out
19 had followed

3 *If*-sentences type 3

1 If Mark hadn't woken up late, he would have got up on time.
2 If he'd got up earlier, he would have had time to plan his trip.
3 If he'd had time to plan his trip, he would have remembered to check the water.
4 If he'd remembered to check the water, the car wouldn't have broken down.
5 If the car hadn't broken down, they wouldn't have had to push it for hours.
6 If they hadn't had to push the car for hours, then they wouldn't have missed the party.

4 Building skills: summarizing

Waterworld: This movie is set in a post-apocalyptic future world where most land is now underwater. As it opens, we meet the Mariner (Kevin Costner), who sails the ocean alone, always searching for fresh water. He soon finds himself unhappily giving protection to Helen and the child Enola. This small girl unknowingly carries the secret of the route to dry land in the form of a map on her back. Attacking the three of them time after time are the evil 'smokers'. These Hell's Angels on water burn oil, smoke and generally behave badly towards everyone else. After many dangers, the smokers are destroyed, and the heroes find the paradise of dry land.

Armageddon: This movie is set in the days before a huge asteroid is due to hit Earth. It opens with the information that it happened 65 million years ago and could happen again. From this, we move to NASA's discovery that it is going to happen again. The only answer is a nuclear explosion deep inside the asteroid to blow it to pieces. The only people who can drill the necessary hole are a wild group of oil drillers led by Harry Stamper (Bruce Willis). The story follows them through to the explosion at the last possible moment. To do this, Stamper has to die, but the asteroid is destroyed and Earth is saved.

5 Wordfield: the environment

Across

1 chaos	6 ice	12 green
3 climate	8 power	13 fusion
4 gas	10 tidal	14 source

Down

2 atmosphere	7 coast	11 tonne
5 avoid	9 region	

6 Technical options

True: 1, 4, 5, 7
False: 2, 3, 6, 8

6 MODERN WAYS TO WORK

1 Vocabulary

A Job title: customer relations officer

1 customer contact	4 challenging
2 repetitive	5 independent
3 regular hours	6 responsible

B

1 I'm doing a secretarial course.
2 I've just got a business studies qualification/qualification in business studies.
3 I applied for lots of different jobs.
4 Being friendly is an important part of the work.
5 I have to do everything accurately.
6 It is amazing how complex today's world of work is./Today's world of work is amazingly complex.
7 My new job is challenging in many different ways.
8 Training is now more flexible than it used to be.

2 Building skills: taking notes on reading

BSG Solar: General:
Type of organization: *private, family-owned firm*
Director: *Barry S Good*
Head Office in: *Oxford* Founded: *21 years ago*

Changes:	21 years ago	Now
Staff:	3	550
Centres:	1	57
The Oxford centre:	workshop, store, small office	just offices
Type of business:	gas central heating systems	solar heating systems

3 Present progressive and present perfect

3 has been supplying
4 have become
5 have fitted
6 has also won
7 has been upgrading/(has upgraded)
8 have been looking

4 Simple past and present perfect

3 've just finished
4 took
5 Have ... given
6 ('ve) had
7 've passed
8 started
9 didn't
10 Didn't ... do
11 was
12 began
13 've put
14 haven't

5 Wordfield: work

(siehe Seite 20)

6 Problems with verbs

1 ~~is taking~~ = takes
2 ~~do~~ = are/'re doing
3 ~~am liking~~ = like
4 ~~travelled~~ = was travelling
5 ~~will~~ = is going to have
6 ~~work~~ = have worked / have been working
7 just go = has / 's just gone
8 ~~have been knowing~~ = have known
9 ~~doesn't~~ = won't
10 ~~would offer~~ = offered

7 Technical options

A

2 What were the men doing when the accident happened? – They were installing a CCTV camera.
3 Where did the accident take place? – It took place on a London construction site.
4 Why did the scaffold lean over at a sharp angle? – Because a concrete transporter hit it.
5 Why did Barry fall from/off the scaffold? – Because he wasn't wearing a safety harness.

B

1 safety harness
2 hard hat
3 tower scaffold
4 CCTV camera
5 concrete transporter
6 ambulance

7 GOING GLOBAL

1 Vocabulary

A

1 Verb	Noun	2 Noun	Adjective
globalize	globalization	freedom	free
solve	solution	redundancy	redundant
transmit	transmission	strength	strong
develop	development	weakness	weak
require	requirement	independence	independent
employ	employment	competition	competitive

B

1 really strong
2 has developed rapidly
3 solve the problem
4 are not free to ask for better conditions
5 (data) transmission costs very little

2 Wordfield: globalization

1 profit
2 fruit
3 goods
4 trade
5 consumers
6 price
7 cheap
8 brand
9 supply
10 producers

3 Building skills: writing a comment

A

1 While
2 On the one hand,
3 On the other hand,
4 As a result,
5 Therefore,
6 However,

B *(freie Lösung)*

4 The passive: describing a process

1 All the car parts are delivered to the factory just in time for use.
2 The parts are taken straight to the production line.
3 The body is put together separately from the rest of the car.
4 Then the engine and all the other parts are mounted in the body.
5 At the end, everything is checked very carefully by quality controllers.
6 Finally, the finished cars are loaded onto transporters and are distributed all over the world.

5 The passive: questions

2 Have travel dates been agreed with Stephen yet?
3 How many units are going to be ordered?
4 Will a larger order be placed before Christmas?
5 Will this first order be sold by all of our shops?
6 Which shops will be asked to sell them?
7 Will this person be paid for by B of B?

6 Passive with modals

2 No, but they should be agreed soon.
3 1,000 ought to be ordered.
4 No, a larger order needn't be placed before Christmas.
5 Yes, it could be sold by all of our shops.
6 All shops might be asked to sell them.
7 Yes, this person will have to be paid for by B of B.

7 Problems with passives

1 ~~requiring~~ = required
2 ~~offered~~ = been offered
3 ~~can bought~~ = can be bought
4 ~~by you~~
5 ~~catched~~ = caught
6 ~~from~~ = by
7 ~~made from~~ = made of
8 ~~It said~~ = It is said

8 Technical options

1 c The Link provides a short route between Sweden and Denmark without taking a ferry.
2 e Today, Mark Sutton is reporting live from the island of Satholm in the Baltic Sea.
3 h The Link is made up of four sections, including a 4-kilometre-long road and rail tunnel.
4 g The tunnel joins the Kastrup peninsula in Denmark to the artificial island of Peberholm.
5 d The Link has two decks, an upper deck for road vehicles and a lower one for trains.
6 b The suspension bridge itself connects Peberholm to the Swedish mainland near Malmö.
7 f The two pylons that support the highest part of the bridge are 204 metres tall.
8 a The company that runs the Link expects about 13000 vehicles to use it every day.

8 FINDING A JOB IN THE EU

1 Vocabulary

1 is studying tourism
2 do a period
3 require students
4 chooses the UK
5 SEC specializes in
6 doesn't give the name
7 aren't paid
8 can make a contribution
9 pay a fee to get
10 emails Lisa the name

2 Building skills: writing a CV

1 Personal details
[1] Name, [2] address, [3] date and place of birth, [4] nationality, [5] daytime phone number, [6] email address (X sex; X marital status)

2 Interests and skills
X References
✓ Cycling and camping
✓ English and Spanish
X LAN parties
✓ EU class C driving licence
X Martin-Luther-Grundschule
✓ Member Red Cross
✓ MS Office

3 Gerund or infinitive?

A

Infinitive	Gerund	Both
would prefer	dream of	begin
afford	admit	continue
decide	deny	hate
expect	enjoy	intend
hope	finish	like
promise	imagine	love
stop	mention	prefer
want	practise	start

B

1 ... have promised to arrive on time.
2 ... have dreamed of working abroad.
3 ... can't imagine winning a lot of money.
4 ... would prefer to stay at home on Friday evening.
5 ... have begun/started to learn/learning French.
6 ... have to stop to get some money.

4 Vocabulary

1 [1] recommend, [2] mixed
2 [1] threatening, [2] corruption
3 corrupting
4 [1] responsible, [2] perception, [3] advisory
5 [1] advise, [2] recommend, [3] to interfere
6 [1] interference, [2] perceptive

5 Building skills: qualifying opinions

1 as far as I can see
2 It is absolutely clear
3 I get the impression that
4 the opposite is true
5 On the whole, I suppose that
6 There can be absolutely no doubt
7 This fact seems to suggest that
8 On the contrary, the fact is

6 Wordfield: word completion

A

1 corruption
2 interference
3 undemocratic
4 bureaucrats
5 perception
6 European Commission
7 national governments
8 legislative power
9 Council of Ministers
10 member state

B

1 ¹ European Commission, ² legislative power
2 ¹ Council of Ministers, ² member states
3 ¹ bureaucrats, ² national governments, ³ perception

7 Technical options

1 X	6 A	11 W	16 S	21 O
2 P	7 D	12 E	17 H	22 N
3 M	8 T	13 U	18 K	23 Q
4 V	9 C	14 Y	19 J	24 R
5 G	10 B	15 F	20 L	25 I

9 SOCIAL CHALLENGES

1 Vocabulary

A

Section A	Section B
1 imperfect	7 inaction
2 untidy	8 misunderstood
3 irresponsible	9 indirect
4 disprove	10 inattention
5 impossible	11 misuse
6 disbelieve	12 increase

B

1 ¹ use, ² misuse
2 ¹ irresponsible, ² responsible
3 ¹ action, ² inaction
4 ¹ decreases, ² increases
5 ¹ perfect, ² imperfect
6 ¹ impossible, ² possible

2 Participle clauses 1

2 When Tracy Parr was growing up in Sandpoint, Idaho, she learned that various family members enjoyed a little gambling.
3 On reaching her 18th birthday, she immediately drove with her boyfriend, Carl, to the nearest casino.
4 While playing every machine in the place that evening she lost $5 - a small price for a lot of fun, she thought.
5 Before leaving the casino to go home that night she had already become a gambling addict.
6 While spending more and more time at the casino in the following months she sometimes won but usually lost - and could never stop.
7 After stealing money from work to feed her addiction she nearly went to prison. / She nearly went to prison after stealing money from work to feed her addiction.
8 She thought there was no escape from gambling before joining a group called Gamblers Anonymous which showed her the way out.

3 Participle clauses 2

Dr Louisa Piper is a psychologist *trained* as a therapist and now *specializing* in the area of family problems. She helps family members *having* difficulties in their relationships. She says the problems *facing* them are often caused by outside stresses. For example, she often sees parents *forced* to work very long hours to earn enough money. That can badly affect children *growing* up in this lonely environment. The personal problems *created* by such pressures come in many forms. She gives as an example one family *badly damaged* in this way. There is an 18-year-old daughter recently *taken* to hospital with severe anorexia. There is also a 15-year-old daughter *staying* out late at night and *spending* time with known troublemakers. And there is a 10-year-old son too *frightened* to leave the house at all. Piper is now setting the family challenges *designed* to bring them together. For instance, Sunday evening has become a 'fun family time' *requiring* them all to spend time together on a shared family activity.

4 Articles

1 a	9 a	16 the	24 the
2 x	10 a	17 x	25 x
3 x	11 x,	18 the	26 x
4 x	12 a	19 the	27 x
5 a	13 an	20 x	28 a
6 x	14 a	21 a	29 the
7 the	15 x	22 a	30 x
8 x	16 the	23 x	31 the

5 Wordfield: social challenges

A *(siehe Seite 20)*

B

1 campaign	4 addiction
2 childcare	5 politician
3 relatives	6 demonstration

6 Technical options

1 sceptical older customer	4 worried waiter
2 cook	5 satisfied younger customer
3 washer up	6 customer adviser

10 MULTICULTURALISM

1 Building skills: describing illustrations

(Lösungsvorschläge)
In the foreground in the middle there are two boys. They are laughing. There is a fruit stall on the left. The stall holder is selling fruit to some customers. You can see a church or maybe town hall with a clock tower in the background. In the foreground on the left there is a black man with a shaved head. On the right in the foreground a man with long hair and a woman are buying something at a grocery stall. A girl is with them. There are lots of people in the middle distance. They are all walking through the market. One of them is a Sikh man in/wearing a turban. We can also see a Muslim woman wearing a hijab. Behind the stall holder on the left there is a woman in a sari.

2 Connectors

1 whose
2 After
3 before
4 However
5 and
6 and
7 because of
8 as
9 In fact
10 because
11 by
12 on account of
13 in which
14 As a consequence
15 that

3 Reported speech: statements

1 ... told reporters that the Spanish government was doing all it could to stop illegal immigrants, but that they couldn't do the job alone. He added that the EU had to help them.
2 ... said that Spain needed some skilled immigrants, but that unfortunately the illegals were almost all unskilled. He pointed out that most couldn't even understand Spanish.
3 ... thought that the anti-immigrant feeling in Spain had been made much worse by the media, which always exaggerated/ (exaggerates) the number of people who were/ (are) coming here.
4 ... emphasized that people thought that African immigrants just wanted to come to Spain to have a better life, but saw it as a humanitarian problem. He concluded by saying that the fact was/ is that these people had/ have no life at all where they came/ come from.

4 Reported speech: questions

1 asked when ... was founded
2 wanted to know what the main role ... is
3 wondered if/ whether ... had to come
4 asked whether the agency's head office was
5 wanted to know (in) how many countries the agency had an office in.
6 enquired what the biggest problem facing the refugee agency was.

5 Reported speech: requests

1 told the driver to switch off the engine.
2 asked him to get out of the cab.
3 requested the man to give him his driver's license and other documents.
4 ordered the Mexican to open the doors at the back of the truck and not to touch anything.
5 instructed the driver to unload some cases and (to) show him what was behind them.
6 told the man not to put his hands in his pockets but to keep them where he can see them.

6 Wordfield: multiculturalism

1 immigrant
2 attitude
3 Colombian
4 ethnicity
5 fashion
6 demographer
7 Hispanic
8 ancestry
9 uniformity
10 megastar
11 popularity

Key word: multicultural

7 Technical options

1 surface buoy
2 electronic systems
3 antenna
4 'sea-side'
5 acoustic transducer
6 radio signals
7 anchors
8 data
9 earth's surface
10 seismographic stations
11 tsunami information
12 coastal communities

11 CRIME

1 Vocabulary

A

1 terrorism
2 armed robbery
3 manslaughter
4 rape
5 graffiti-spraying
6 shoplifting
7 murder
8 burglary
9 mugging
10 drunk driving

B *(freie Lösung)*

2 Grammar: adverb order

1 I'm afraid the police don't patrol the streets *very frequently*.
2 Liberal commentators *always* claim that poverty causes crime.
3 Harsh punishment *seldom* stops people from committing crimes.
4 I enjoy a good crime novel *now and then*.

5 (*Usually*) There is *usually* an increase in street crime at Christmas.
6 Unfortunately, people *sometimes* leave valuables in their cars.
7 (*Often*) There's *often* no point in reporting trivial crimes to the police.
8 You should lock the doors *every night*.

3 Grammar: word order

1 *Tomorrow* the prime minister is opening the new Marsh Prison in Leeds (*tomorrow*).
2 Prime ministers do not *usually* open prisons, but this is a particularly important occasion.
3 Marsh Prison is *completely* different from traditional prisons.
4 *Unlike traditional prisons*, Marsh Prison is more like a hotel than a fortress.
5 *For example* the cells are bigger and have a separate toilet and shower like in a hotel.
6 Each cell is occupied by *just* one prisoner.
7 And prisoners will *only* spend twelve hours a day in their cells.
8 Prisoners will *usually* spend the rest of their time doing a useful job or job training.
9 *Of course*, some conservatives complain that prisoners are not on holiday.
10 But supporters say that we must find an answer to the problem of suicide in *traditional prisons*.

4 Building skills: giving a talk

(Antworten in dieser Reihenfolge von oben nach unten.) 7, 5 ,8 ,9, 4, 6, 1, 2, 3

5 Wordfield: crime

1 deterrent	5 shoplifter	9 robbery
2 corrupt	6 murder	10 sentence
3 bribery	7 NYPD	11 tolerance
4 merciless	8 racism	12 rape

M	E	R	C	I	L	E	S	S	B	O	L	G	A	V
I	U	T	M	W	E	N	O	O	B	X	F	A	E	S
E	N	R	P	R	O	L	S	E	N	T	E	N	C	E
A	B	V	D	S	H	U	H	A	D	E	S	V	I	S
H	T	H	I	E	N	T	O	L	E	R	A	N	C	E
I	U	F	S	K	R	E	P	E	A	G	S	I	O	T
B	R	I	B	E	R	Y	L	C	E	D	D	Y	R	S
V	O	C	H	E	S	A	I	P	L	U	M	B	R	E
O	B	E	A	T	H	S	F	E	M	O	I	S	U	T
B	B	P	I	L	M	S	T	P	A	R	N	Y	P	D
M	E	F	I	E	G	E	E	A	C	L	O	T	T	R
N	R	I	D	E	T	E	R	R	E	N	T	D	A	T
P	Y	S	C	H	P	R	I	O	F	S	I	D	A	X

6 Technical options

1 earpiece	6 end call
2 left/right selection	7 scroll
3 menu	8 keypad
4 clear display	9 power switch
5 call	

12 FUTURE LIFE, FUTURE LIVING

1 Vocabulary: definitions

A

1 boycott	7 ingredient
2 offspring	8 astonishing
3 current	9 calf
4 announce	10 vast
5 derive from sth.	11 prematurely
6 ban	12 onset

B

1 ban	4 current
2 derive from	5 prematurely
3 offspring	6 astonishing

2 Vocabulary: collocations

1 farm animals	6 clone farming
2 emergency talks	7 science fiction
3 EU officials	8 dairy herd
4 health laws	9 animal suffering
5 Holstein calf	10 lung infection

3 Multiple matching: speakers and statements

1 H	3 A	5 C	7 G
2 B	4 D	6 F	8 E

4 Building skills: translating English into German

(Lösungsvorschläge)
1 Leider haben wir bis jetzt bei der Kontrolle des Klonens wenige Fortschritte gemacht.
2 Einige wertvolle Möbelstücke wurden beim Brand/im Feuer beschädigt.
3 Die Nachrichten über das Klonen von Menschen sind erschreckend.
4 Sie werden viele Informationen über das Klonen im Internet finden, aber vieles davon ist Unsinn.
5 Nicht alle Wissenschaftler, die gerade mit dem Klonen experimentieren, sind verantwortungsvoll.
6 Mein Arzt/Die Ärztin hat mir gesagt, ich soll in Zukunft weniger essen und mich mehr bewegen.
7 Bob studiert Biologie, seitdem er lesen kann.
8 Die Universität hat die Versuche gestoppt/unterbunden, da/weil mehrere Wissen-

schaftler/innen gerade dabei waren, gegen das Gesetz zu verstoßen.
9 Man sagt, dass das menschliche Leben sich durch medizinische Fortschritte vollkommen verändern wird.
10 Man befürchtet, dass die zunehmende Digitalisierung zu einem vollständigen Verlust der Privatsphäre führen könnte.

5 Grammar problems

1 meeting
2 pairs of scissors
3 who
4 coming
5 didn't go
6 have been
7 are flying
8 have been waiting
9 the role of Violetta wonderfully
10 in the flats in Station Road
11 were waiting
12 cycle
13 is going to work
14 would you do
15 slices of ham
16 sheep
17 had come
18 had to do
19 shoes
20 was made

6 Wordfield: word snakes

A tendency to get illnesses(,) such as cancer and diabetes(,) is programmed by a person's DNA. Food poisoning is often caused by somebody's carelessness between the farm gate and the supermarket shelf.

7 Technical options

1 It is hoped that the use of robots will reduce the cost of medical care.
2 Robotic surgery means less pain and much shorter recovery times for patients.
3 Advances in robotic surgery will cause radical changes in heart operations.
4 In conventional heart bypass operations the patient's rib cage must be opened with a 30 cm long incision.
5 No human hand can match the steadiness of a robotic arm.

Technical Topics

1 INTERNAL COMBUSTION ENGINES

1 A 4-stroke internal combustion engine

1 camshaft
2 spark plug
3 fuel intake
4 exhaust valve
5 intake valve
6 cylinder head
7 combustion chamber
8 cylinder block
9 piston
10 crank case
11 crankshaft
12 crank chamber

2 Parts of an engine

1 c
2 g
3 d
4 e
5 a
6 h
7 f
8 b

3 An engine quiz

1 b
2 a
3 b
4 c
5 c
6 a
7 c

4 Testing useful engine power

1 torque
2 dynamometer
3 unemployment
4 [1] mass, [2] strap
5 [1] brake, [2] wheel
6 formula
7 brake horsepower
8 [1] watts, [2] 750

2 ELECTRICITY

1 Electricity distribution

A

1 housing
2 voltage
3 generate electricity
4 factory
5 overland powerline
6 power station
7 transmit
8 pylon
9 transform
10 transformer station

B

1 generate
2 power stations
3 overland powerlines
4 pylons
5 transform
6 voltage
7 transformer stations
8 transmit
9 housing
10 factories

2 Electrical circuits

1 b
2 d
3 a
4 b

3 Circuits

1 volt
2 ohm
3 electric
4 switch
5 ammeter
6 battery
7 voltage
8 resistor
9 current

The key word is 'voltmeter'.

4 An accident report

1 f The accident took place in the kitchen of a house in Manor Road, Birmingham.
2 d Harry Driver was using an electric drill to drill a hole into a wall.
3 e Harry rested his left hand on a metal kitchen cabinet while he was drilling.
4 g An electrical fault in the drill electrified the conductive metal parts of the drill.
5 c The 3-pin plug of the drill had no earth terminal as it had broken off.

6 h The current found its path to earth through Harry's body and the cabinet.
7 a Harry was badly hurt by the electric shock and he had to be rushed to hospital.
8 b Doctors now say that Harry will recover but he could easily have been killed.

3 TOOLS

1 Names of tools

A

1 pipe wrench
2 pipe bender
3 oil can
4 wire stripper
5 digital multimeter
6 smoothing plane
7 hex key
8 mason's hammer
9 pruning shears
10 trowel

B

1 pruning shears
2 pipe bender
3 hex key
4 trowel
5 wire stripper
6 mason's hammer
7 digital multimeter
8 oil can
9 pipe wrench
10 smoothing plane

2 Which tool for which job?

1 a saw
2 a hacksaw
3 a wire stripper and a screwdriver
4 a hammer drill and a masonry bit
5 a hex key
6 a socket wrench
7 a chain saw
8 a lathe
9 a hammer
10 some metal shears

3 Which tool for which person?

1 carpenter: saw, plane, wood chisel
2 electrician: insulated screwdriver, wire strippers, multimeter
3 mechanic: socket wrench, hex key, oil can
4 gardener: shredder, pruning shears, chain saw
5 bricklayer: cold chisel, trowel, mason's hammer
6 plumber: pipe wrench, hacksaw, pipe bender

4 MATERIALS AND THEIR PROPERTIES

1 Objects and materials

1 aluminium piston
2 leather jacket
3 steel girder
4 ceramic beer mug
5 wooden pallet
6 plastic petrol can
7 glass windscreen
8 rubber tyre
9 cardboard box
10 brass screw
11 paper bag
12 cotton T-shirt

2 Describing materials

A

	Noun		Adjective	
	English	**German**	**English**	**German**
1	brittleness	*Brüchigkeit*	brittle	*brüchig*
2	conductivity	*Leitfähigkeit*	conductive	*leitfähig*
3	malleability	*Verformbarkeit*	malleable	*verformbar*
4	elasticity	*Dehnbarkeit*	elastic	*dehnbar*
5	plasticity	*Plastizität*	plastic	*plastisch*
6	porosity	*Durchlässigkeit*	porous	*durchlässig*
7	hardness	*Härte*	hard	*hart*
8	transparence	*Durchsichtigkeit*	transparent	*durchsichtig*

B

1 [1] Brittle, [2] hard
2 Rubber
3 [1] conductivity, [2] conductive
4 elasticity
5 Plastic
6 [1] malleability, [2] malleable
7 [1] transparent, [2] brittle
8 [1] porosity, [2] porous

3 Looking at the text

1 h 2 f 3 g 4 b 5 j 6 c 7 a 8 d 9 e 10 i

5 ENERGY

1 Energy sources

1 fossil fuels (coal, oil, gas)
2 solar energy
3 hydroelectric energy
4 wind energy (wind generators)
5 geothermal energy
6 nuclear energy

2 Energy consumption in the USA

1 C 2 A 3 B

A [1] 2007, [2] five, [3] 51 %, [4] electricity, [5] LPG, [6] kerosene
B [1] energy, [2] space heating, [3] appliances, [4] 14 %, [5] consumption/energy, [6] air-conditioning
C [1] 2005, [2] 22 %, [3] transport, [4] industrial, [5] four

3 How a hydroelectric power plant works

A

1 control gate
2 intake
3 reservoir
4 dam
5 transformer
6 powerhouse
7 power lines
8 generator
9 outflow
10 turbine
11 penstock

B

(freie Lösung)

6 SAFETY

1 Hazards in a workshop

1 into	7 to	13 on to	19 on
2 on	8 for	14 on	20 without
3 out	9 down	15 under	21 of
4 with	10 against	16 across	22 in
5 around	11 of	17 on	23 of
6 in	12 on	18 in	24 to

2 Safety first

Person	Appearance	Activity	Unsafe behaviour
welder	white girl; early 20s; short brown hair; long-sleeved pink shirt	standing at workbench; welding L-shaped workpiece; writing with left hand	doing two things at the same time; not wearing goggles or gloves
window-cleaner	white man; mid-20s; black hair; long-sleeved brown sweat-shirt, blue jeans	cleaning outside of window from tower scaffold	not wearing hard hat or safety harness; leaning out too far from scaffold
man in doorway	black man; late 20s to early 30s; short black hair; light brown short-sleeved shirt, dark brown trousers	carrying large cardboard box in front of body	cannot see where he is going

3 Signs puzzle

Across

1 hat
3 toxic
5 goggles
8 caution
9 harmful

Down

1 harness
2 explosive
4 flammable
6 radioactive
7 biohazard

4 Mediation

1 You mustn't smoke, eat or drink in this part of the factory.
2 You should only use the yellow walkways because of forklift trucks.
3 All fire extinguishers are inspected once a month.
4 Visitors to the building site must wear a hard hat.
5 Most accidents in factories are caused by people ignoring the safety rules.
6 Tools that are no longer needed must be cleared away immediately.
7 Emergency exits must be kept free at all times.
8 All accidents must be reported to the plant management immediately.

7 SUPPLYING THE GLOBAL MARKET

1 Logistics

A

1 haulage
2 management
3 supply
4 information
5 delivery
6 user
7 distribution
8 allocation
9 assembly
10 collection
11 analysis
12 transport

B

1 are transported
2 allocation of work
3 [1] analysis, [2] delivery problems
4 [1] assemble, [2] supplied/(delivered)
5 collect and deliver
6 information

2 Containers

1 barrel of oil
2 tube of glue
3 jar of jam
4 bottle of ketchup
5 can of paint
6 sack of potatoes
7 box of screws
8 packet of seeds
9 tub of ice-cream
10 stick of lipstick

3 A supply chain

1 E Fruit on the tree
2 G Bananas cut off tree
3 C Transport to farm by road
4 F Washing and labelling
5 A Packing in boxes
6 K Loading in Caribbean
7 B Transport to Europe by sea
8 I Bananas at logistics centre in Europe
9 J Transport to retailer by road
10 H Point of sale
11 D End user/consumer

8 TECHNICAL JOBS

1 Jobs

1 d
2 b
3 g
4 h
5 a
6 c
7 e
8 f

2 Places of work

1 electrical workshop – electrician
2 car repair shop – mechanic
3 woodworking shop – carpenter
4 computer repair shop – IT technician
5 bicycle repair shop – bicycle mechanic
6 metalworking shop – lathe operator

3 Talking about jobs

1 personal day	5 company pension plan
2 utility company	6 health insurance
3 life insurance	7 self-employed
4 working conditions	8 training allowance

4 Job descriptions

1 The company is looking for qualified electricians to work on its construction site in Berlin.
2 Successful applicants will have a minimum of two year's experience in this type of work.
3 Bonuses are/will be paid for good work in addition to a generous salary and help with accommodation.
4 You will install complete electrical systems in large buildings such as office blocks.
5 As a heating technician, you will be expected to install, maintain and repair heating systems in offices and private homes.
6 You you will work closely with the architect/s and site management to achieve the highest standard of work.
7 Heating technicians and electricians must be able to work reliably on their own initiative.
8 Success candidates will be (a) good team worker(s) who is/are able to cooperate with others.

9 LOW-ENERGY TECHNOLOGY

1 Sankey diagrams

A

1 e In Sankey diagrams, the width of the arrows is proportionate to quantity or mass
2 h Such diagrams are often used to show the useful energy or efficiency of machines.
3 b Sankey diagrams were developed by the Irish engineer Matthew Sankey in 1898.
4 f Sankey's original diagram showed the kinetic energy generated by a steam engine.
5 d The Sankey diagram on page 186 illustrates energy gains and losses within a building.
6 c The first arrow shows the loss of primary energy caused by extraction, transport and conversion.
7 a The first arrow at the bottom shows a small energy loss of 5 % in the heating system.
8 g According to the diagram, the gains of solar energy amount to some 79.6 %.

B

1 d   2 b   3 c   4 a

2 An eco-house

1 eco-house	8 solar cells
2 two	9 sun
3 windows	10 wind turbine
4 double-glazing	11 electricity
5 walls	12 heat pump
6 roof	13 ground-source
7 insulation	14 recycling bins

3 Condensing boilers

1 condensing boilers	5 water vapour
2 heat exchanger	6 waste pipe
3 flue gases	7 energy efficiency
4 preheating	8 energy costs

4 A solar water heater

A

1 tank
2 insulation
3 hot water at top of tank
4 cold water at bottom of tank
5 cold water returns to solar collector
6 cold water reheated in solar collector
7 hot water rises to tank

B

(freie Lösung)

10 EASING THE LOAD

1 Force-distance substitution

1 The principle of force-distance substitution was first described by Archimedes.
2 'Force-distance substitution' reduces the 'work energy' needed to do a job.
3 In a block & pulley setup, the less the force, the longer the rope.
4 One end of the rope is attached to the weight, the other end is pulled.
5 The invention of the block & pulley made much bigger sailing boats possible.
6 A block & pulley setup must be attached to a fixed point such as a beam.
7 A setup with just one pulley does not reduce the required force at all.

8 A setup with four pulleys reduces the force by a factor of 4.
9 Block & pulley systems are used to raise and lower elevators.
10 Double pulleys are used to reduce the number of separate pulleys required.

2 Jumbled words

1 [1] hydraulic, [2] liquid, [3] oil
2 [1] force, [2] cylinder, [3] load
3 [1] advantage, [2] divide, [3] piston head
4 [1] substitution, [2] travel, [3] larger

3 Adverbs and prepositions

1 In	9 from	17 by
2 with	10 as	18 within
3 of	11 by	19 into
4 between	12 of	20 up
5 in	13 into	21 of
6 of	14 in	22 down
7 by	15 in	
8 of	16 of	

4 Passive

1 are usually lifted
2 [1] is divided, [2] must be applied
3 [1] has to be exerted, [2] can be reduced, [3] has to be travelled, [4] is increased
4 [1] is being loaded, [2] is called
5 [1] are raised and lowered, [2] is powered
6 [1] is translated, [2] easily be calculated, [3] is divided

11 DATA COLLECTION AND STORAGE

1 Solid state storage

1 e	3 b	5 g	7 f
2 d	4 h	6 c	8 a

2 Letter to the editor

A

1 traded	7 social networking
2 gathered	8 undetectable
3 build up	9 sifted
4 predict	10 controlling
5 massive amounts	11 tested
6 in my view	12 potential for abuse

B

1 invisible
2 undetectable
3 predict, forecast
4 trade, buy and sell
5 social networking
6 massive amounts, huge quantities
7 in my opinion, in my view
8 store
9 abuse
10 control

3 Questions on the letter

1 Information is not only gathered and stored by governments and companies, but also shared and even traded on a massive scale.
2 This does not have to be particularly dangerous in democracies with functioning parliaments, independent courts and a free press.
3 unmanned aerial vehicles (UAVs); radio-frequency identification microchips (RFID); closed circuit television (CCTV); trail of data from clicks on web pages, phone calls, use of credit cards and ATMs
4 Because it is intended to hold up to 49 different items of information about everyone living in the country.

4 Collecting data

1 closed-circuit television camera; unmanned aerial vehicle
2 ID card; diagram of an eye; dog tag
3 mobile phone
4 chip
5 ATM

12 ROBOTICS

1 Industrial robots

1 up of	4 [1] of, [2] to, [3] through, [4] in
2 [1] into, [2] with	5 [1] to, [2] in, [3] of
3 [1] to, [2] of	6 [1] from, [2] in, [3] around

2 Humanoid robots

A

2 shoulder	5 hand	8 ankle
3 elbow	6 hip	9 foot
4 wrist	7 knee	

B

1 To go up stairs, the robot would use his feet, ankles and knees.
2 To open a door, he'd/would use his hand, wrist and elbow.
3 To bend down, he'd/would use his knees and hips.
4 To file a piece of steel, he'd/would use his shoulder, elbow, wrist and hand.

5 To saw a length of wood in half, he'd/would use his shoulder, elbow, wrist and hand.
6 To walk across a room, he'd/would use his knees, ankles and feet.

3 Robot basics

1 a	3 b	5 a	7 c
2 c	4 b	6 b	8 c

4 Word snake

According to statistics issued by the US Department of Labor, increased automation, most importantly the growing use of industrial robots, has caused the huge majority of job losses in American manufacturing industries over the last twenty years or so. In spite of media hysteria about jobs moving to Asia and eastern Europe, in fact job migration has played a much smaller role than usually thought.

Unit 1, 6 A, Wordfield: city life (WB S. 19)

S	A	P	A	R	T	M	E	N	T	W	S	K	Y	L	I	N	E	I	K	L	M	P	O	S
C	W	K	K	L	E	Z	T	R	A	S	S	B	G	M	J	S	H	O	P	P	I	N	G	K
O	X	N	N	E	I	G	H	B	O	U	R	H	O	O	D	S	T	B	K	E	P	T	H	Y
M	S	C	W	O	I	G	P	R	E	N	Y	U	L	Q	D	C	H	U	Y	T	Z	F	B	S
M	W	A	D	H	A	T	T	R	A	C	T	I	O	N	K	R	M	I	O	R	I	E	L	C
U	C	P	N	B	M	T	W	V	X	K	V	C	B	R	U	O	L	L	N	A	B	S	T	R
N	E	I	Z	O	B	E	D	O	W	N	T	O	W	N	I	W	O	D	M	F	P	T	K	A
I	M	T	I	R	I	N	R	G	H	T	J	K	Y	E	U	D	E	I	G	F	J	I	R	P
T	K	A	L	O	R	E	M	B	U	S	I	N	E	S	S	E	Z	N	O	I	U	V	N	E
Y	P	L	W	U	E	R	V	I	O	M	Z	R	K	T	N	D	R	G	M	C	E	A	W	R
J	T	E	I	G	F	G	H	C	U	L	T	U	R	A	L	A	W	A	E	H	D	L	I	N
M	A	S	G	H	E	Y	T	P	F	I	O	N	T	W	G	T	R	A	D	I	T	I	O	N

Unit 3, 5 A, Wordfield: the media (WB S. 26)

X	C	E	L	E	B	R	I	T	Y	T	Z	T	E	X	T	I	N	G	R	P	U	P	I	K
V	W	Q	A	J	K	L	Y	X	E	F	R	Q	A	W	E	S	R	D	C	R	V	R	N	P
I	G	P	O	P	U	L	A	R	I	G	E	M	V	I	E	W	E	R	B	E	D	O	F	R
T	M	D	S	B	M	P	L	W	L	R	A	P	L	O	K	I	J	N	M	S	U	G	H	O
I	N	T	E	R	A	C	T	I	V	E	L	R	C	O	M	E	D	Y	E	S	X	R	C	D
E	D	R	F	V	B	G	T	Z	H	N	I	U	J	I	M	O	P	Y	A	W	Q	A	E	U
Q	Y	M	O	B	I	L	E	E	S	D	T	R	T	O	F	F	L	I	N	E	U	M	F	C
M	N	B	G	V	F	V	F	E	D	C	Y	E	M	X	D	E	W	S	A	Q	I	M	D	E
D	E	D	A	U	D	I	E	N	C	E	V	R	O	M	E	S	S	A	G	E	K	E	D	R
R	F	V	B	C	D	E	S	W	X	M	U	J	V	Z	H	N	B	R	F	W	B	L	O	G
E	N	T	E	R	T	A	I	N	I	N	G	R	I	W	P	U	I	B	G	V	R	C	E	W
G	C	H	R	J	I	C	E	U	T	Z	B	Q	E	D	O	C	U	M	E	N	T	A	R	Y

Unit 6, 5, Wordfield: work (WB S. 38)

Q	T	E	M	P	O	R	A	R	Y	P	S	C	T	E	C	H	N	I	C	I	A	N	X	A
R	W	E	D	C	X	S	W	A	C	L	A	A	S	D	B	N	Y	I	K	N	F	P	M	R
E	C	O	N	T	R	A	C	T	L	Q	L	Z	E	X	P	E	R	I	E	N	C	E	B	O
C	E	R	X	H	V	C	D	B	E	Y	E	Q	S	X	C	D	E	R	F	V	T	G	X	U
E	Z	E	Q	T	I	O	Z	V	R	B	S	P	R	O	D	U	C	T	I	O	N	H	Q	T
P	Y	M	S	E	T	M	N	M	K	A	P	T	E	D	L	M	N	T	Z	U	I	R	E	I
T	T	P	T	F	Z	M	U	B	S	R	E	T	W	O	R	K	P	L	A	C	E	F	E	N
I	F	L	G	A	H	I	J	E	X	F	R	D	W	E	F	T	G	Z	H	U	J	I	C	E
O	V	O	B	C	N	T	M	N	E	T	S	C	W	D	P	R	O	S	P	E	C	T	S	M
N	C	Y	Z	T	M	M	I	E	D	G	O	V	V	F	R	T	G	B	Z	H	N	Z	H	N
I	X	E	H	O	J	E	K	F	C	B	N	F	Z	I	N	T	E	R	V	I	E	W	D	C
S	Y	R	J	R	U	N	O	I	W	A	I	T	E	R	M	N	B	G	F	V	D	C	S	X
T	Q	E	M	Y	I	T	L	T	R	U	Z	U	H	N	E	M	P	L	O	Y	M	E	N	T

Unit 9, 5 A, Wordfield: social challenges (WB S. 50)

A	G	O	V	E	R	N	M	E	N	T	W	X	W	M	B	P	M	A	B	A	N	D	O	N
P	E	S	X	T	A	I	K	L	T	P	R	E	S	S	U	R	E	D	Y	N	Q	P	W	P
E	L	E	C	T	I	O	N	M	B	W	E	R	L	I	E	T	R	M	W	V	N	O	R	E
T	V	R	W	C	H	S	I	S	O	C	I	A	L	I	Z	E	G	O	E	I	P	L	S	M
R	M	E	A	N	S	T	S	G	E	R	S	P	L	C	B	N	R	V	N	O	M	I	T	O
E	D	L	U	S	D	R	A	D	D	I	C	T	I	O	N	T	X	E	C	L	Y	C	M	T
L	Y	A	P	O	L	U	V	M	W	E	K	L	E	Q	T	E	C	M	B	E	P	I	E	I
I	K	T	L	C	N	C	P	O	L	I	T	I	C	I	A	N	M	E	W	N	T	E	I	O
G	M	I	A	I	P	T	W	R	C	A	Y	Q	W	E	P	C	M	N	T	C	R	S	Z	N
I	Y	V	M	E	Y	U	N	C	A	M	P	A	I	G	N	E	L	T	S	E	W	I	E	A
O	I	E	X	T	E	R	B	R	I	D	E	Z	T	G	U	I	C	I	D	R	U	G	A	L
N	A	I	L	Y	W	E	H	G	M	E	D	I	A	O	P	L	H	E	W	O	X	K	C	L
A	C	H	I	L	D	C	A	R	E	X	N	D	E	M	O	N	S	T	R	A	T	I	O	N